ANTHROPO ME...

Designing to Fit the Human Body

∎ ∎ ∎ ∎ ∎ ∎ ∎ ∎ ∎ ∎

John A. Roebuck, Jr.
Roebuck Research and Consulting,
Santa Monica, California

MONOGRAPHS IN HUMAN FACTORS AND ERGONOMICS

Alphonse Chapanis, *Series Editor*

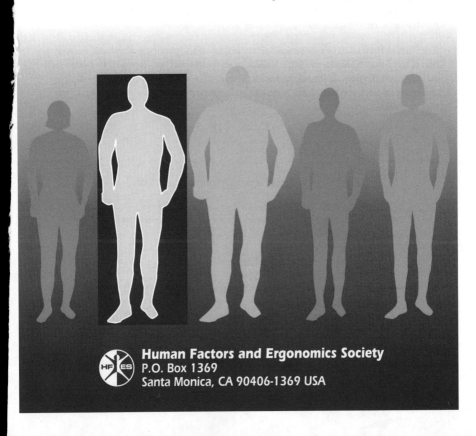

Human Factors and Ergonomics Society
P.O. Box 1369
Santa Monica, CA 90406-1369 USA

Additional copies of this book may be obtained from the Human Factors and Ergonomics Society for $15.00 per copy for members and $20.00 per copy for nonmembers. Add $5.00 for shipping and handling and California sales tax if applicable. Discounts apply on purchases of five copies or more; contact the Society at the address given above.

The Human Factors and Ergonomics Society is a multidisciplinary professional association of more than 5200 persons in the United States and throughout the world. Its members include psychologists, designers, and scientists, all of whom have a common interest in designing systems and equipment to be safe and effective for the people who operate and maintain them.

Library of Congress Cataloging-in-Publication Data

Roebuck, John Arthur, 1929–
    Anthropometric methods : designing to fit the human body /
by John A. Roebuck, Jr.
       p. cm.
    Includes bibliographical references and index
    ISBN 0-945289-01-4 : $15.00
    1. Human engineering.   2. Anthropometry.   I. Title.
TA166.R62   1993
620.8'2--dc20   93-16975
                                 CIP

CONTENTS

ACKNOWLEDGMENTS

I am deeply indebted to Alphonse Chapanis for his careful editing and many suggestions for improvements, as well as for his continuing encouragement and favorable comments that kept me going when the possibility of completion of this document seemed bleak. I also gratefully thank the two reviewers who labored extensively over the details of one of the drafts. Some of their helpful comments have been incorporated almost verbatim. I have not specifically credited these sources, but they should recognize what they wrote.

I thank the Human Factors and Ergonomics Society for giving me the opportunity to organize and present the material in this book and for publishing it. The extensive efforts of Lois Smith of the central office in reviewing and dealing with the shortcomings and long development process also need acknowledgment.

There are many other colleagues who generously offered material and permission to publish it, much more than I could include. My family also deserves much credit for putting up with my time away from duties of father and husband for the many hours that were needed to prepare this book.

Chapter 1

INTRODUCTION

This book reports on a technological revolution occurring in the methods of anthropometry, or the measurement of human beings. In it, I describe what these methods were like before the revolution, how they are changing, and what they may be like in the future. As you read, you will learn about the traditional ways of anthropometry and why they continue to be important: for understanding how past data were obtained, for maintaining comparability with data from future surveys, and for forecasting new design criteria. But more important, throughout the book I highlight and advocate many new methods for measurement, analysis, and design applications. You will see how the development of these new methods was spurred by the advent of computers, new opto-electronic measurement devices and other capabilities of the electronic age, and by new procedures of engineering practice, such as concurrent engineering.

Included in this overview of the methods of anthropometry are descriptions of how this science can beneficially influence the practice of human factors/ergonomics in the design of products that can be used readily and safely. I start by covering methods for taking anthropometric measurements, summarizing statistical data, performing analyses, and preparing reports. Then I provide examples of the applications of anthropometric data to the design and evaluation of work spaces, small tools, controls, components, and clothing. My purposes are to open doors for further inquiry into advanced methods, assist readers in performing simple estimations of missing data, and reveal the benefits of the recommended procedures for planning measurements or performing applications.

What Is Anthropometry?

Anthropometry is the science of measurement and the art of application that establishes the physical geometry, mass properties, and strength capabilities of the human body. The name derives from *anthropos,* meaning human, and *metrikos,* meaning of or pertaining to measuring. Measurement of humans can be important for many applications, including criminology, medical practice, and personnel selection. However, I will emphasize design applications here, consider the measurements most useful for design, and show how they are used for that purpose.

Anthropometric methods are among the basic working tools for the analysis and development of engineering design requirements by human factors and ergonomics professionals. Considerations include the wide range in sizes, proportions, mobility, strengths, and other factors that define human beings physically. Human sensing and performance capabilities are in part related to these physical characteristics, so anthropometric concerns also influence many aspects of human factors related to physiology and the psychology of comfort and perception. For example, anthropometry helps human factors/ergonomics specialists describe three-dimensional (3D) spatial locations of the eyes so as to determine what can be seen and thereby identify obstructions that limit vision and cause mistakes.

Anthropometry helps to (1) evaluate postures and distances to reach controls, (2) specify clearances separating the body from hazards such as surrounding equipment, and (3) identify objects or elements that constrict movement. Anthropometry also deals with many quantities related to biomechanical analyses of forces and torques during manual materials handling, operator fit in vehicles, accommodation comfort, and general human performance.

Anthropometry can assist in the design of tools and handles that can be readily grasped and operated. It may help clothing designers produce better-fitting garments and make it easier for clothing buyers and military quartermasters to decide how much and what sizes of clothing to buy.

Anthropometry is frequently a hidden consideration in many studies that involve subjective judgments. For example, it may provide numerical data permitting the comparison of a person's body dimensions to seat heights, breadths, depths, and support angles. Studies have shown that there are ranges of these dimensions that correlate closely with feelings of comfort or discomfort according to the activity performed in the seat.

In summary, anthropometry is a major component in the total systems point of view that is a hallmark of good human factors or ergonomics practice.

History

Anthropometry is an outgrowth of physical anthropology. As first conceived more than 200 years ago, it was used in an attempt to distinguish among races and ethnic groups of humans, to identify criminals, and to aid in making medical diagnoses. More recently, it has become useful in industrial settings and is identified with the development of engineering design requirements and the evaluation of modern vehicles, work sites, equipment, and clothing (Roebuck, Kroemer, and Thomson, 1975). Evaluations of cockpits and clothing were strongly supported and determined by military needs during and following World War II (Hertzberg, 1955). However, a great many applications of anthropometry today are to commercial and civilian equipment, vehicles, and clothing (CAD Modelling, 1992; Czaja, 1984; Roe, 1993; Sanders and Shaw, 1985). Although studies in the area of anthropometry are infrequent and lack prominence in academic anthropology, technical papers sometimes appear in the *American Journal of Physical Anthropology.*

I will not dwell on the long and rich history of anthropometry but will focus on methods used in the recent past and emphasize those planned for the near future. Additional information is available for those who are interested in the history of the science (e.g., Hertzberg, 1955; Kroemer, Kroemer, and Kroemer-Elbert, 1994; Roebuck et al., 1975; White, 1978).

Aside from being a developing science, certain aspects of the subject matter of anthropometry qualify it as a *historical science,* much like geology. In the same way that continents move almost imperceptibly, individuals and groups of people constantly undergo change. Anthropometric surveys, whether large or small in scale, are historical events and can never be repeated in exactly the same way, even on the same people, because the people will have changed. These changes are caused by normal physiological diurnal variation or aging processes. It is very likely that some of the individuals surveyed will later become unavailable for measurement. That is why populations are frequently identified by year of measurement as well as by occupation and ethnic group. Body dimension survey reports serve as benchmarks against which new survey data can be compared. In a sense, they are technical "fossils" that help us trace and predict the microevolution of groups of humans. In that way, they provide bases for forecasts suitable for design criteria. (Forecasting is described in Chapter 5.)

The Influence of Electronic Modeling and New Measurement Technologies

Currently, technological innovations are changing the ways in which anthropometry is used in engineering applications. Among these innovations are computer modeling of people as substitutes for living humans in computer-aided design (CAD) for human factors applications, and the use of new electronic imaging methods for measurement. Anthropometric measurement and application methods are currently undergoing significant revolutions in concepts as a result of new technologies. At the same time, there is greater emphasis on the systems engineering point of view and a need for integrating diverse approaches into a general, unified one.

Enhancements in computer graphics that facilitate computer-aided design have produced new demands for methods of 3D visualization and statistical manipulation of body sizes and shapes. They have resulted in widespread attempts to develop graphical computer models of human body forms and functions. Such models are fast becoming a key feature in human factors/ergonomics applications involved with a popular new design approach called *concurrent engineering* (also called *simultaneous engineering;* see Boyle, Ianni, Easterly, Harper, and Korna, 1991; Majoros, 1990; Roebuck, 1991). A major goal of concurrent engineering is to complete engineering analyses before spending a large percentage of project funds on the construction of physical mockups, prototypes, or products. Ergonomists today cannot rely as heavily on the responses and fit of living subjects in mockups; instead, they must incorporate models of human responses and size variations into electronic models of humans.

These developments have focused attention on past and current deficiencies of anthropometric data gathering, reporting, and application methods and have created new demands for more comprehensive, integrated data. Notable examples of needs include 3D measurements of body surface contours and landmarks, locations of internal joint centers of rotation (see Chapter 2), and determination of interjoint link lengths and orientations. More data are also needed on the effects of changes in orientation, pressures of external surfaces on body flesh, environmental effects, clothing shape, and new concepts for body support.

To date it has been common to have different sets of data and models for each application area (e.g, work space or clothing). However, the development of computer models and data-handling technologies offers new opportunities for using large, central mathematical databases and more integrated, comprehensive representations of the human form that are potentially useful for several purposes, such as the design of clothing, work space, tools, and equipment.

Those who attempt to construct human models invariably feel a need for more data than are available from most surveys. These data are needed to adequately define body shape in three dimensions and to describe ranges of movement for joints. Furthermore, even when a great deal of contour data are known (up to 5000 points), it has generally not been at the key cross-sections desired (passing through joints and at specified percentages of distance between joints) or related to internal links and joint centers in the same way from subject to subject. As a result, the contour data cannot be readily analyzed using conventional statistics.

These conditions have led researchers to look for new approaches, such as typical sets of equations that describe general form functions common to many different people and standard sets of internal coordinate systems related to joint centers and vectors connecting them. Modelers thereby hope to more completely specify body shape, size, and postures without incurring excessive cost to gather, analyze, and publish data. Such research is likely to improve our understanding of how the geometry of human bodies may be defined in terms of statistical variables and in terms of functional mechanisms.

Benefits in many fields may result, such as the enhancement of sports performance and the design of personal protective gear, clothing, medical prostheses and medical equipment, tools and assembly jigs, and vehicle interiors.

The evolution of new computer modeling techniques has been accompanied by parallel developments in new measurement technologies. Some of these are lasers, stereo video, structured light, flying-spot light beam, magnetic resonance imaging (MRI), computer-aided tomography (CAT) scanning, special X-ray methods, ultrasonic visualization, sonic digitization, and movement measurement methods. Imaging concepts and goals are changing, in many cases blending into those of anthropometry. Most of these new methods couple computers to sensors in ways that produce digitized data, points, and pixels located in three-dimensional space. These produce outputs that are distinctly different from older, single-dimensional or two-dimensional ones. Though not obvious, behind the two-dimensional image seen on a computer monitor may be a wealth of data on size, shape, and location never before available.

These measurement capabilities complement the new data needs, but they pose problems in comparing and understanding the data produced by the older, manual methods. Among the potential solutions to these problems are new approaches to data gathering, methods for data compression, and development of highly capable software to deal efficiently with "new clouds of data."

Knowledge and Skills Required for Anthropometry

As you read this book, you will learn of the types of knowledge and skills that are required to perform this kind of work successfully. A brief preview follows.

Traditional measurement requires some knowledge of anatomy — especially the locations, names, and shapes of bones and muscles — and an understanding of how to read measurement scales, measure weights, and handle instruments. For the advanced technologies, an understanding of the principles of electronics, lasers, photography, and video devices is necessary. For planning measurement surveys, for data reduction and analysis, and for forecasting and estimating, you will need introductory knowledge of statistical principles. The greater your depth of training in statistical principles, the better you can deal with the many problems involved and the higher the level of creativity and complexity you can attempt with the hope of success. Successful planning also requires some experience in dealing with the organization of time and processes in an efficient and effective order.

You can enhance survey reports if you have artistic skills in life drawing, the ability to depict measurement equipment and its use in a graphic fashion (generally with line drawings), and a sense of pleasing arrangements for layout of text and illustrations. Of course, good language skills (grammar, punctuation, spelling) and facility in writing scientific material, including proper reference citations, are highly valuable for clear communication.

Applications typically require knowledge of mathematics (including algebra, geometry, and trigonometry), mechanical aspects of physics, and some mechanical engineering principles and practices. You have to be able to read engineering orthographic drawings and to understand concepts of mass properties, force, and torque. A talent for visualizing geometric relationships and for performing elementary design work for planning mockup evaluations is beneficial. Applications work may require abilities to perform hands-on construction of models, special measurement devices, and full-scale mockups from a variety of materials.

Because measurements involve dealing with people, including touching them and directing their movements to assume certain postures, you must be able to explain your activity in a credible manner. Developing a friendly relationship with subjects while maintaining a professional attitude will ensure acceptance and cooperation.

In order to gain the advantages of networking with other professionals — such as encouraging a good interchange of data, advancing the technology, and facilitating the collection of information — you need to have a helpful, friendly, and honest approach with peers. Finally, an ability to speak in public will help you present your results to customers and members of the engineering and human factors/ergonomics community.

Chapter 2

PLANNING FOR MEASUREMENTS

A fundamental requirement when selecting measurements and measurement methods is to plan ahead to satisfy users of the data that will be produced. This is done by (1) imagining future applications, (2) performing task analyses on future uses of the data, and (3) asking potential users what they need, either face to face or by means of a questionnaire. After the list of perceived needs is compiled, creative methods to estimate some dimensions (described later) may be developed to help limit the number and kind of dimensions to be measured. Here, I plea for "big picture thinking" or, more correctly, the systems approach. This approach looks at a wide range of interacting factors in society, technology, and individual design projects to determine how best to integrate them into usable systems in the future.

Most anthropometric measurements represent samples taken at one point in time (a *cross-sectional survey*); rarely are individuals tracked in a series of measurements as they age (a *longitudinal survey*). As a result, sequential surveys will reveal changes in means, variabilities, correlations, and proportions of body parts that may be caused by attrition from death, illness, disinterest, aging, selection, or dietary changes. Also, there may be significant changes in the proportions of different racial or ethnic groups surveyed at different times that may affect averages in body proportions.

These factors should be taken into account not only when deciding on sampling procedures but also when assessing the accuracy and meaning of anthropometric data. This is especially important with regard to age brackets because of the relatively rapid changes that occur during youth or extreme age.

Elements of a Measurement Plan

Deciding on what to measure depends to varying degrees on many aspects of planning for anthropometric measurements. For example, you need to perform such mundane activities as finding suitable facilities, obtaining suitable subjects, preparing paperwork to recruit subjects and for the legal release of data, purchasing or building instruments and other equipment, and obtaining the services of those who will measure and analyze the data. Other needs are logistic and nearly independent of what is measured: scheduling transport if several sites are considered; arranging for housing, feeding, sanitation, and thermal comfort of subjects; and scheduling and distributing the work of the measurers. Finally, checking data before entry into records, recording data efficiently, and writing, editing, and publishing reports are essential to communicate the results.

Facilities

The site for measurements must include private space for disrobing; adequate room for stands, jigs, chairs, desks, and other furniture; and storage for instruments and supplies. The workload and time required at each station (if more than one) should be organized for a balanced and smooth flow of subjects through the facility. To reduce confusion caused by audible reading of instructions and measurements, I recommend using separate rooms when more than one subject is being measured at the same time.

Equipment

The measuring team must obtain or have available anthropometric instruments and chairs, tables, jigs, and fixtures in sufficient number for each measuring site, plus spares in the event items are damaged in handling. Computers are preferable for checking and recording data because measurements recorded by hand will generally have to be entered into a computer at some point. Typewriters may be useful for some types of paperwork. Forms, recording sheets, diskettes, and other supplies may also be needed.

Checking Software and Procedures

Every measurement made with instruments by human beings is subject to errors. Measurers sometimes misread scales, transpose digits, or err in judgment when rounding readings. Subjects may make inadvertent motions, or measurers may be inconsistent in the amount of pressure they apply to body parts in making measurements. Gavan (1950) summarized studies of consistency of anthropometric measures prior to 1950 and provided details on other problems of measurement. Churchill, Bradtmiller, and Gordon (1988) provided a table of expected and acceptable variations in measurement for each dimension. Gordon and Bradtmiller (1992) also summarized studies on the accuracy of measurements made during the most recent major survey, that of U.S. Army personnel during 1987–1988.

In general, it is desirable to perform each measurement twice and to compare the results to see if the readings are the same or acceptably close. With modern computers and appropriate software, some types of errors can be detected by comparing a reading with expectations of the extreme range for typical comparative populations. Software may also accumulate data as measuring proceeds and develop a continually updated prediction of expected population statistical extremes (e.g., 2 or 3 standard deviations) for each dimension being measured.

As data are accumulated during the measurement process, software may also be used to calculate dispersion of values around average trends (regressions of one dimension on one or more others). A convenient statistic for describing such dispersions is the standard error of estimate. Some of these software applications are described in the report by Churchill et al. (1988), which includes a helpful historical summary of the use of computers for the analysis of anthropometric survey data. The report also explains (with examples) the use of regression formulas to test for outliers, or deviant measures to be expected in a population of measures.

Personnel

Each measuring site typically requires two people: one to record and one to conduct measurements. If complicated adjustments are required, a third technician may be needed. It is best if a female measurer works with female subjects and a male conducts measurements of male subjects, especially when measurements are made in sex-sensitive areas. A receptionist can be an asset for admitting and checking in subjects according to a schedule of appearance times, for dealing with paperwork, and for answering questions at the beginning of a measuring process. Subject selection is a key concern and may require several recruiters.

Training

Measurers need to be trained in proper techniques and tested to assure the principal investigator that all are using the same techniques. To ensure consistency among measurers requires hours of practice and consistent monitoring of results. The principal investigator also needs to check that each measurer will obtain the same results when measurements are repeated.

The time required for training will depend on the number of new skills to be learned and the background of the personnel. Reference to previously published reports and conferences with knowledgeable persons in the field are the only guides for estimating time requirements.

With technology available today, preparing a videotape of the measurement methods is more feasible and cost-effective than in the past and can expedite training. Videotaped records also serve as effective supplements to written documentation of methods used in the survey and can be of enormous help in the standardization of data. Video records were used in the 1988 survey of U.S. Army personnel (Gordon et al., 1989a, 1989b), and I recommend such records for all large surveys.

Scheduling

The number and relative complexity of measurements should be divided equitably among the measuring teams to make efficient use of their time, to ensure a smooth flow of subjects, and to prevent delays. Commonly, the measurer and recorder alternate tasks after a suitable period (say, an hour) to reduce fatigue and boredom. Scheduling should take into account procedures for ensuring health and safety. When direct-contact methods are used, provisions should be made to prevent the transmission of disease. For example, instruments were wiped with alcohol before each use during the 1988 Army survey, and subjects were given disposable paper slippers and washable shorts.

Administrative Concerns

In organizations performing anthropometry, as in any human organization, there are administrative needs to resolve problems of pay (unless volunteers are used), lines of authority, permission to use buildings and rooms, scheduling of work hours, and so forth. Of course, the major function of administrators is to ensure that the planning efforts are carried out through effective and timely actions by all involved in the surveys.

What to Measure?

Those who plan anthropometric surveys are faced with conflicting goals in deciding what parts and attributes of the human body to measure. A goal of industrial applications is workplace design, which requires data on body segment lengths and heights, some breadths, and some depths, but very few circumferences. By contrast, clothing design and size distribution decisions require many circumferences and distances along surface contours but few lengths or heights. Physiological studies may require data on volumes, densities, and areas of the human body. Computer modeling of the human form for work space design and manual materials handling requires dimensions that can aid in locating joint centers of rotation and interjoint link lengths relative to skin surfaces, and offsets in relation to consistent, 3D coordinate systems.

No matter what kinds of measurement devices or media are used, the question of what to measure for engineering anthropometry *must* include postures. These typically include a standard standing posture, a standard upright sitting posture, and certain postures that permit maximum reach measurements of the arms and legs. As I will explain later, future needs for the location of joint centers may dictate several different postures (typically three) for each joint that can be flexed or extended, in order to locate effective centers of joint rotation.

Ideally, a full set of contours for the entire body should be scanned in several postures to provide details of body cross-sections so that joint centers of rotation can be derived. Models incorporating a full set of contours for the whole body may prove useful for many different applications. Such ideals have rarely been achievable within constraints of time, money, and available technology. If contour data are not gathered, measurers should obtain many more depths, breadths, and offsets than is typical of current practice.

Historical Practice and Measuring Standards

Standard measurements are needed for comparative purposes and for forecasting trends. Ideas about which dimensions should be standard have gradually changed along with purposes for anthropometric measurements. There has been a major shift in goals for the use of data away from purely scientific studies of differences among peoples in various parts of the world and toward engineering applications. Even the desired measurements for engineering applications have changed since the reports of military anthropometric surveys by Hertzberg, Daniels, and Churchill (1954) or Hertzberg, Churchill, Dupertuis, White, and Damon (1963). For this reason, subsequent reports differ in some particulars, and none can be said to include a so-called standard list.

For the most part, the survey reports done by and for the U.S. Air Force present a high quality of documentation that can be used for teaching about commonly used measurement methods and instruments. They frequently include text and illustrations of techniques with line drawings and photographs. Examples of pages from such a report are discussed in Chapter 4.

A more readily accessible commercial publication, which also includes many photographs, is the *Anthropometric Standardization Reference Manual* (Lohman, Roche, and Martorell, 1988). However, this book emphasizes measurements of interest for sports medicine and performance, rather than for the design of work space or clothing.

The foregoing discussion of differing approaches raises the question, "What are the accepted standards for measurement naming, measurement selection, and measurement methodology?" An extensive and authoritative source for titles of landmarks and measurement methods was written in German by Martin (1928) and later revised (Martin and Knussman, 1988; Martin and Saller, 1957). Though now out of print, it may be available in some university libraries. In later years, certain general approaches to establishing names for dimensions have evolved, and many names appear consistently throughout the literature on physical and engineering anthropometry (Hertzberg, 1968). Few international and national conferences have been convened to seek consensus on naming conventions and to make recommendations about standard measurement methods and preferred number of dimensions in surveys. The latest in the United States was reported by Hertzberg (1968). His article is recommended reading for those interested in this aspect of the field, even though it was written more than two decades ago and much has changed in measurement and application technology in the meantime.

In a useful (and massive) collection of data from worldwide sources, Garrett and Kennedy (1971) directly compared descriptions and names of similar measurements on a measurement-by-measurement basis, but they did not attempt to recommend standards for future use. A later compilation of data in Volume II of the three-volume set of the *Anthropometric Source Book* published by NASA (Anthropology Research Project staff, 1978a, 1978b, 1978c) also provides typical names and brief descriptions of anthropometric measurements. Goals of economy and simplicity of presentation of these extensive tables of data led to careful selection of a single title for all similar measurements, with the result that this document may be considered a de facto standard for names of dimensions, at least in the United States. Even so, meetings are needed today to seek greater consensus on traditional measurements and to focus on the major impact of computer-generated human modeling, use of lasers, and other electronic imaging in anthropometrics.

Although it had a different focus and agenda, a 1991 workshop on the general topic of electronic human modeling began to address some of these issues (CSERIAC, 1991). However, that workshop was mainly concerned with medical imaging and software communication standards rather than anthropometry for design. There remains a need for the integration of traditional and new technologies in the context of anthropometrics, and for the establishment of a permanent committee to oversee and suggest new standards as technology changes rapidly in the electronic age. The Society of Automotive Engineers (SAE) has held committee meetings in the 1990s for the purpose of setting computer human modeling standards. The agreements resulting from these meetings could also affect standards for naming anthropometric dimensions, performing measurements, and selecting preferred minimum lists of measurements. Eventually, these activities may lead to a new congress, with wider representation, that will recommend worldwide standards for anthropometric measurements.

Appendix B presents illustrations and names of many of the standard, single-dimensional anthropometric measurements that are frequently used in traditional anthropometry for engineering applications. These illustrations were drawn from reports prepared for the 1988 survey of U.S. Army soldiers (Donelson and Gordon, 1991; Gordon et al., 1989a, 1989b). They also appear in the measurer's handbook prepared for training the measuring team for that survey (Clauser et al., 1987). These documents include illustrations of *land-*

marks (key features marked on the body prior to measurement) that often identify locations of underlying bone features.

Although many measurements are common to all past large-scale military surveys, some notable exceptions can significantly influence applications of the data to design. To indicate the nature of the problems one might encounter, I present two examples: Waist Height and Buttock-Heel Length. (Throughout this book, the convention for naming specific dimensions is to capitalize the first letter of each significant word in the title.)

Waist Height

Either of two easily confusable measurements may sometimes be erroneously listed simply as Waist Height. To be correct, the dimension name should indicate which of two common landmarks was used for the Waist Height measurements. One is the *navel* (called *omphalion* in some reports); the other is the *natural indentation* (NI), the place where the middle portion of the trunk is narrowest (as seen from the front or back) and where the circumference is generally smallest. Sometimes the natural indentation cannot be located on very obese persons, in which case the measurer must make an arbitrary decision about its location. On military personnel, it generally can be found by inspection. If not, one may select a height half the distance between the tenth rib and the top of the pelvis (iliocristale). An alternative method for locating the NI is to place around the middle of the trunk an elastic cord that has a round cross-section, adjust its length to apply moderate tension, and then release the tension. The cord will seek the height with the smallest circumference. This height can then be marked and the circumference at that height measured with the tape.

In several past surveys, either one or the other (but usually not both) of the above-described Waist Heights has been measured (Anthropology Research Project staff, 1978b). However, both were measured on U.S. Army personnel in 1988, thus providing an indication of their relative sizes. For males, the difference in height between these two commonly reported waist height measurements was 6.83 cm; although this difference is not negligible, it is not large enough for determining from inspection of the data whether the measurement is to the navel or to the natural indentation.

If measurements to the waist are made on a sitting subject, the dimension name should have an associated modifier (Sitting) as well as one describing the point of measurement on the body, as correctly listed in Appendix B (120 and 121).

Less commonly, the term *Waist Height* is given to the measurement that is more correctly called *Iliac Crest Height* (or *Iliocristale Height,* as shown in Appendix B). It is measured to the top of the pelvis, and its average height is nearly the same as average navel height in military personnel.

Incidentally, in Volume II of the extensive NASA *Anthropometric Source Book* (Anthropology Research Project staff, 1978b), detailed descriptions of Waist Height measurement methods are contained on pages 3–25, along with the survey titles, dates, number, and types of persons measured, as well as other particulars of each population sample. They are not on page 70, where you might expect to find them among the alphabetically listed and illustrated measurement descriptions. A statement on page 70 says only that the measurement is at "the height of the waist level."

Buttock-Heel Length

Another, more subtle type of problem relating to definition of measurements illustrates how critical it is to understand postures used in measurement and the ultimate use of data (what they were intended to measure). As an example, I use the measurement variously called *Buttock-Leg Length, Buttock-Heel Length, Functional Leg Length,* or *Total Leg Length.* It may be measured in a variety of ways with different results (Garrett and Kennedy, 1971). For designing computer-generated models and drafting manikins, a theoretical upright sitting posture, with legs fully extended forward at the knee (as shown in Figure 1a), would be desirable. Note that the upper and lower legs are in alignment, and the sum of distances from heel to hip joint (approximately equal to Trochanteric Height) could be subtracted from the Buttock-Leg Length to determine the horizontal location of the hip joint. In fact, the bent-knee posture shown in Figure 1b is more realistic when the back is upright.

Hertzberg et al. (1954) found that many men cannot actually achieve the extended posture in Figure 1a when sitting with a hip angle of 90 degrees. I estimate the mean of the reported measurements to be as much as 2.3 cm (0.9 in) longer than the theoretical length and the standard deviation to be 0.64 cm (0.25 in) greater.

As an alternative approximation to the theoretical posture, some later surveys have selected the posture shown in Figure 1c (Clauser et al., 1987, Gordon et al., 1989a, 1989b). However, even this posture introduces an error in average length of perhaps 2.2 cm. (0.87 in), depending on the angle of the leg from horizontal. Because the theoretical posture cannot be measured as a single dimension on most populations, alternative methods are needed to derive it, and these generally require a combination of two or more measurements.

Figure 2 illustrates two potential approaches, each using three measurements. In each of the two approaches, Idealized Buttock-Heel Length is determined by adding Buttock-Knee Length (A) to a newly defined distance called *Flexed Knee-Heel Length, Standing.* The latter is calculated as a difference

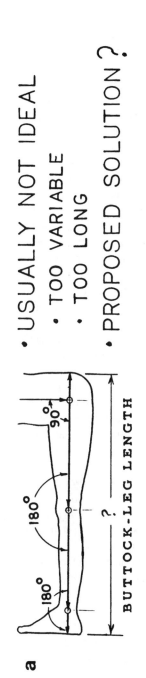

- USUALLY NOT IDEAL
  - TOO VARIABLE
  - TOO LONG
- PROPOSED SOLUTION?

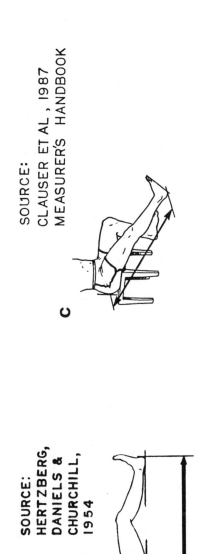

Figure 1. Theoretical ideal (a) and actual (b and c) postures for measuring Buttock-Leg Length (Roebuck, 1991).

between two other dimensions. In one case, the difference between Stature and Kneeling Height (both labeled B) determines Flexed Knee-Heel Length, Standing. In the second case, the difference between Trochanteric Height and Trochanteric-Knee Length, Kneeling (both labeled C), determines Flexed Knee-Heel Length, Standing. (Kneeling Height has been measured only rarely in past surveys and does not appear in Appendix B.) Trochanteric-Knee Length, Kneeling, is a newly defined dimension that I propose for future surveys.

Another factor to be accounted for in sitting measurements is that lack of weight on the heel pads and joints and subtle leaning postures involved in stable standing orientations can introduce small differences in overall lengths of distances like Trochanteric Height. As I noted previously, posture is an important part of measurement definition, often because of gravitational loads on the flesh and joints. When a subject is in a posture to measure the Functional Leg Length (Figure 1c), the distance from heel to trochanteric landmark is likely to be longer (perhaps 0.5 to 0.7 cm) than Trochanteric Height. As the need for accuracy increases, much more careful and detailed attention will have to be paid to effects of posture and gravitational load on distances between landmarks. Further discussion of these concerns appears in Chapter 7.

The example of discrepancies in Buttock-Heel Length measurements points out the importance of understanding how measurements were obtained. This knowledge will enable you to decide whether measurement methods are sufficiently accurate and whether it is necessary to estimate the probable error and make corrections before applying the results to a design. This example also suggests a need for measurements that define joint centers of rotation accurately so that estimates of unmeasured dimensions in alternative postures can be made with confidence.

Recommendations Summary — Traditional Measurements

To sum up, for each population, you must read the descriptions of how the measurements were made. I urge researchers and writers dealing with anthropometry to (1) attempt to use standard methods when possible; (2) accurately describe each measurement method used, especially if it is unusual or if no commonly recognized standard is available; and (3) locate all such descriptions together in reports and handbooks so that they can be readily compared.

New Standards Are Needed

In addition to the traditional, single-dimensional measurements found in past survey reports, a revolutionary change in emphasis is required for the development of computer models. Specific needs have arisen to measure locations of *internal joint centers of rotation*. These may be described as

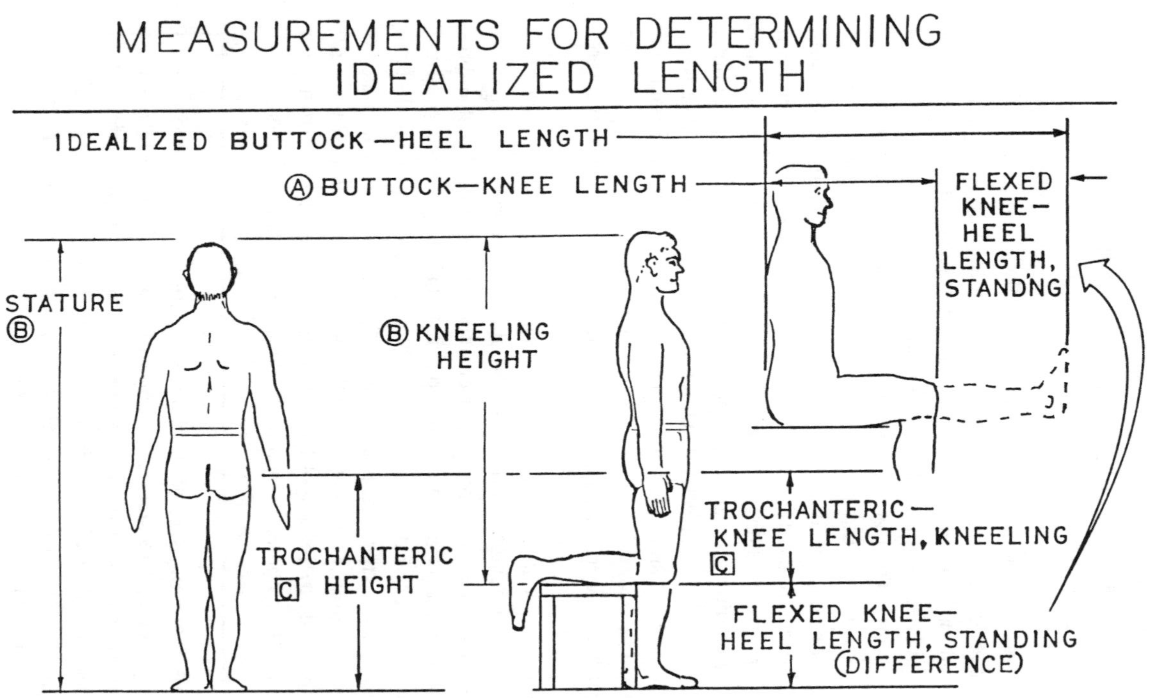

MEASUREMENTS FOR DETERMINING IDEALIZED LENGTH

IDEALIZED BUTTOCK—HEEL LENGTH

Ⓐ BUTTOCK—KNEE LENGTH

FLEXED KNEE—HEEL LENGTH, STANDNG

TROCHANTERIC—KNEE LENGTH, KNEELING Ⓒ

FLEXED KNEE—HEEL LENGTH, STANDING (DIFFERENCE)

Ⓑ KNEELING HEIGHT

TROCHANTERIC Ⓒ HEIGHT

STATURE Ⓑ

Figure 2. *Proposed approach to obtaining Buttock-Leg Length using two measurements (Roebuck, 1991).*

17

either instantaneous, variable locations relative to body segments at different angles of posture, or as locations that remain in constant relation to body segments regardless of postures. These data are needed to accurately place body segments so that standard anthropometric postures and nonstandard, working postures can be simulated.

There is also a need to locate joint centers *from skin surfaces*. This is not a new idea, but its importance is now more fully recognized in light of computer-generated human models used in computer-aided design. Data of this kind would have been useful for the design drawing of layouts and for the early articulated drafting manikin templates that have found widespread use in engineering. (These are discussed in more detail later.) CAD modeling of humans can and should represent real persons and even hundreds of synthetic persons with many different percentiles in each body image. More accurate representations of joints and distances between them will make it possible to perform realistic evaluations of movement clearances and reaches in three-dimensional geometric definitions that become, in effect, "electronic mockups." Effective and efficient evaluations of electronic mockups in terms of anthropometric criteria require computer simulations using "electronic people" — in other words, computer-generated manikins that are accurately sized, shaped, and articulated in accordance with anthropometric data.

Locating joint centers from skin surfaces is necessary because most models are based on internal links that determine where the body segments move to in nonstandard postures. Unfortunately, the majority of past anthropometric measurements have been limited to external lengths, diameters, and circumferences of the skin surfaces. Although many standard landmarks have been related to underlying bone protuberances that, in some cases, indicate the approximate location of joint centers, anthropometers and compasses (p. 29) can be applied only to the skin of living persons, not the bones. To date such measurements have not really measured centers of rotation of joints.

Human factors analyses of workplaces require more than simply a description of the size and shape of people in the standard anthropometric postures. These analyses depend on *predictions* of what people will look like in *nonstandard, application-specific, operating postures* or while relaxed in various types of seats, couches, and other body support devices.

There are two fundamentally different approaches to locating joint centers. One is to locate bony protrusions near the *probable* effective center of rotation. Some examples of landmarks include the trochanteric protrusion (near the hip joint), the lateral femoral epicondyle (near the knee joint), and the lateral malleolus (near the ankle joint). (See the Glossary for definitions of anthropometric terminology). Some past anthropometric surveys have measured *heights* of these points from the floor or distances from some other similar body landmark, but they have seldom measured their distances to other important nearby skin surfaces at the side or in front or back of the joint.

A partial solution to this problem was studied and reported by Dempster (1955), who measured many details of cadaver bone joint configurations, described where joint centers could be located in relation to bone shape details, and derived formulas for estimating distances between effective joint centers, *relative to bone lengths.* These distances he called *links.* However, Dempster did not establish rules for locating links or joints from the outer landmarks measured by anthropometrists.

A second approach is to select key landmarks and measure their relative locations to each other at three or more different postures or flexion angles of the joints. Dempster (1955) described how measurements of this type could be analyzed using the method of Reuleaux (see Glossary) to obtain instantaneous centers of rotation. In one case, he made measurements of the wrist joint centers and angles of rotation on live subjects using the markings and jigs shown in Figure 3.

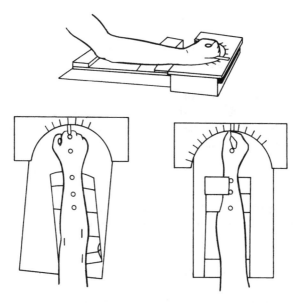

Figure 3. Measurement jig for locating the center of rotation of the wrist on live subjects (after Dempster, 1955).

We now need standard methods for doing these measurements on *all* the joints of living subjects. Unfortunately, it is difficult to make them because skin landmarks move relative to bones as joints are flexed and extended. Jigs and locating devices that maintain minimal displacements relative to bones need to be designed and verified, then specified as standards. If this cannot be done, then the variations in thickness of flesh from bony landmarks need to be measured as a function of angle of posture.

In defining locations of joint centers of rotation, you should consider the ultimate use of the data. For studies of actual joint instantaneous motion (as are needed for the design of prosthetic devices), it is valuable to track the small variations in position that occur at all joints. However, for many engineering applications, it is sufficient and desirable to define an *effective center of rotation* or *design center of rotation* (DCR; or *axis of rotation* in some cases). Sometimes this spot is called the *average center of rotation* or *average joint center.* This terminology, however, does not necessarily mean that an arithmetic mean was actually computed from a series of measurements of locations of joint centers.

What are the characteristics of such a defined location for effective joint centers? Let's consider the knee joint. This joint, as seen from the side, operates in a complex sliding and rotating motion. The instantaneous center of rotation follows a roughly semicircular path. However, to simplify the design of computer manikins and drafting manikins, we need a single point. The location of that point should meet the following criteria:

1. In a standing posture, a manikin should exhibit the full Stature dimension. (Designers of manikins intended only for sitting postures may ignore this criterion.)
2. In a sitting posture, a manikin should exhibit the exact, measured Buttock-Knee Length and Knee Height, Standing. (These dimensions, and others named below with uppercase letters, are illustrated in Appendix B.) If possible, the design should also correctly reflect Popliteal Height and Buttock-Popliteal Length.
3. There should be no change in length between the centers of rotation of the ankle, knee, and hip during simulated leg motions. (This is a convenience for simplifying the design of manikins, not a hard-and-fast rule.)
4. The joint center should be "reasonably located" within the body, in the region of the knee. (This is most critical for drafting templates.)
5. The relative location of the upper and lower leg segments should be correct within acceptable tolerances in both standing and sitting postures, and preferably in other postural conditions. This cannot always be achieved because of bulging and shrinking of muscle tissue and the effects of gravity on living subjects.

In summary, I recommend that locations of joint centers of motion that are intended for use in modeling and design analysis should be derived from considerations of design applications, as well as from actual measurements of body external dimensions.

Floating Dimensions

Many traditional measurements, reported independently, present a real problem to modelers. Consider the Chest Depth, Waist Depth, and Buttock Depth measurements shown in Appendix B. Each of these commonly measured depth dimensions is useful in itself, but there is no dimension that ties them together or anchors them to a common coordinate axis in the anterior-posterior direction. So, when attempting to draw a profile of the body, you do not know how far the back of the waist lies anterior to the buttocks or to the back of the thorax at the nipple height. This problem is common to many other traditional anthropometric dimensions, such as breadths, depths, and circumferences of the limbs. These dimensions are sometimes described as *floating dimensions.*

One way to overcome floating dimensions in the future is to measure all landmarks in a common, three-dimensional coordinate system. Figure 4 defines names and orientations of planes commonly used in anthropometry for the measurement of distances and ranges of joint motion. Also shown are terms for directions and locations of body parts relative to the commonly defined planes and axes. For example, the term *distal* means "away from the central part of the body." Thus, the wrist is distal to the elbow.

Another good practice is to define various local coordinate systems for each limb segment, then relate those to each other at key endpoints. Reynolds (1977), Reynolds, Freeman, and Bender (1978), and Reynolds and Hubbard (1980) have suggested such a system based on specific pelvic landmarks. I prefer selecting joint centers or key bony protrusions near joints as landmarks for defining local coordinate systems. This approach should make it easier to relate all exterior surfaces to internal links, and even to develop reasonably concise mathematical formulas for describing the surfaces. For example, mathematical descriptions would be facilitated by approaches that define locations of landmarks and cross-sections in terms of *percentages of link distances* rather than only in terms of specific incremental dimensions (such as every 2 cm). Such data would avoid much time-consuming guessing and estimating of some significant anatomical relationships that are important for modeling the human body mathematically. Resolution of these issues will shape future directions in anthropometry.

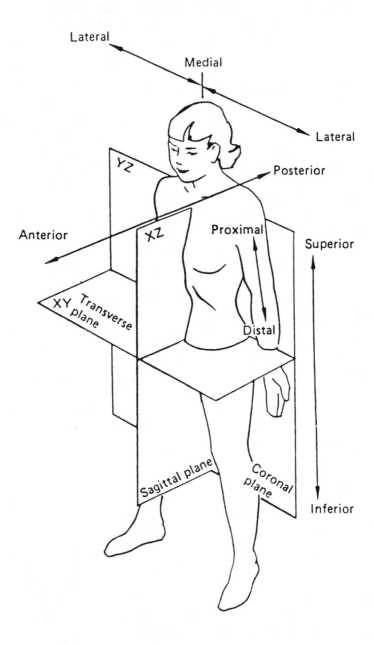

Figure 4. Principal planes for an anthropometric coordinate system and terms of orientation (NASA, 1986).

Ways to Control Potential Increased Costs

Using traditional instruments and techniques to make additional 3D measurements and to define joint locations almost certainly will increase the cost of future anthropometric surveys. One possible cost containment measure is to increase the degree of automation of data measurement and data analysis beyond what is typical today. The rapid growth of computer and sensor technology has made increased automation feasible. What remains is to obtain agreement and to begin to change standard practices that can implement the options. In the following chapter, I will discuss some of these new automation options as well as the traditional methods that must be understood to apply the data from past surveys properly.

Combining Traditional and New Measurements

Anthropometric survey planning should generally include many traditional external dimensions developed by physical anthropologists. Data obtained with traditional methods are needed for tracking secular changes, for relating individual subjects and samples to larger populations, and for scaling up or down in modeling. At the same time, data need to be gathered on multiple postures to determine joint locations using modern scanning and photographic techniques described on pages 43–46.

All of these desirable objectives must be balanced against practical budget and time constraints. I recommend a compromise approach that recognizes different goals for typical, widespread applications and yet seeks dimensions that will support new concepts for computer 3D modeling in a way that can at least partially satisfy many different needs. Traditional anthropometry provides for numerous types of measurements, from those based on feeling resistance of underlying bone to those involving slight pressures. In addition, it does not require line-of-sight access, and the measurements have usually been well defined (although they may vary from one survey to the next), so that anthropologists and ergonomists understand both what the measurements represent and the methods for summarizing and analyzing the data.

Many of the electronic and optical measuring devices show promise of providing new and richer shape descriptions, but problems arise when comparing the traditional with the new types of data. In addition, methods for analyzing these new types of data have not yet been developed or understood. However, if there are to be technological improvements in anthropometry, there must be serious attempts to use and understand the strengths and weaknesses of the newer devices and methods. I am confident that there are those who are willing to develop new definitions of measurements that are appropriate to the new devices and that will become acceptable as standards.

Finally, my reading of history leads me to believe that mathematicians and engineers will develop new mathematical and statistical approaches for summarizing the data in ways that are useful for biometric research and for design applications. In Chapter 3, I emphasize many newer devices and procedures, even though some of them currently lack proof of validity or well-developed methods for dealing with the data they produce.

Nonstandard Measurements

Specific engineering applications (such as described in Chapters 7, 8, and 9) often require nonstandard measurements involving a wide variety of postures and special instruments. In industries such as automobile manufacturing, which have a long history of developing methods, approaches have been worked out and have become accepted practice. In other cases, anthropometry specialists are on their own. They may adapt the general principles underlying standard measurements but go on to devise creative approaches to their work.

Chapter 3

DEVICES AND PROCEDURES
FOR MEASUREMENTS

The great variety of instruments and procedures available for making anthropometric measurements makes it difficult to classify and describe them in any simple, coherent manner. I could try to group them according to the body dimensions and attributes that are to be measured, given that these have strong influences on what devices and procedures should be used. However, available funds, schedules, and prior procurements of instruments also play a part. Additional factors are the constraints of measurement sites, need for mobility, and availability of power sources and supplies for high-technology devices.

I will deal first with devices and associated procedures that are based on simple and fundamental principles, such as direct contact with the body, manual adjustments, and visual reading of analog scales. In many cases, these approaches were the first devised and include fairly versatile, often compactly stowable devices and associated methods that can be carried into jungles and deserts anywhere in the world by anthropologists, without the need for batteries or other electrical power sources. Although often the least costly devices, these may require more time to use than automated devices and systems. In this first grouping I include a few optical devices and methods that depend strongly on manual setup, hands-on measurement, and real-time readout activity. Then I describe some modern versions of devices for direct-contact measurement that require electric power and may involve electronics.

The next major grouping includes devices for indirect measurements. These often involve some degree of automation. Such devices and procedures first capture images by means of various forms of wave energy, such as light, X rays, or sound. The images are then digitized (measured), either manually (e.g., measuring photographs) or by means of electronic devices, perhaps with the use of computers.

Landmarks

Before measurements are made, either by direct contact or by remote (indirect) methods, key sites on each subject's body (called *landmarks*) should be marked. Marking devices should use ink that is safe for the skin, washable, and not subject to smearing during measurements, such as surgical markers.

Figure 5 locates sites of several typical anthropometric landmarks. Detailed descriptions of how each landmark was determined and how instruments are to be applied for each measurement should be prepared as part of the record of the study and (as previously mentioned) for training measurers.

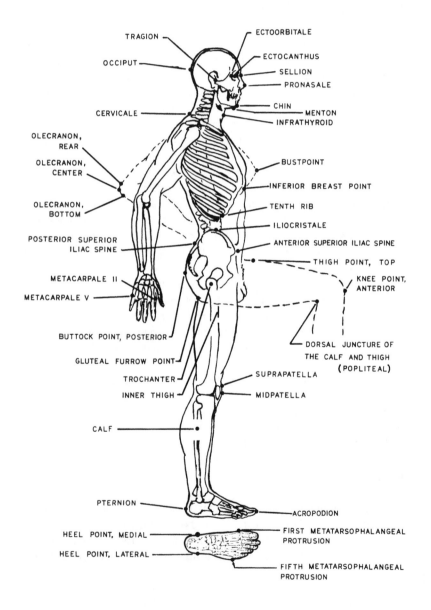

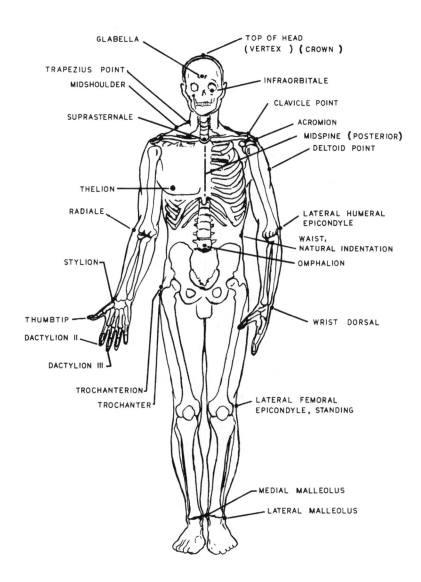

Figure 5. Anatomical landmarks and principal bones (Gordon et al., 1989b, and other sources; human figure modified from Atlas of Human Anatomy *for the artist by Stephen Rogers Peck. Copyright 1951 by Oxford University Press, Inc., renewed 1979 by Stephen Rogers Peck. Reprinted by permission of the publisher).*

Measuring and Recording Size, Shape, and Angles with Manual Anthropological Instruments

Methods that involve direct contact of anthropometric instruments with the surfaces of the body or subjects' clothing (contact methods) or that use on-site readings of optical devices (optical methods) are classified by Roebuck et al. (1975) as *direct methods.* The instruments used are determined primarily by the type of distances (e.g., diameters or circumferences) to be measured.

Linear Dimensions

These measurements are the shortest distances between two points on the body and are usually of greatest interest for the evaluation of work sites. In the past, when linear measurements involved breadths or depths, they were sometimes called *diameters,* but this practice is not recommended (Hertzberg, 1968). Typically, this class of dimensions includes lengths of the long bones and surrounding segments of the arm and leg, breadths and depths of the trunk, and projected dimensions (heights of landmarks from a floor or horizontal offsets from a wall). Past methods of measurement usually did not relate each length dimension to a standard three-dimensional coordinate system, and unfortunately this practice continues in anthropometry.

However, the situation is not entirely hopeless. Typically, a floor or wall has provided an implied reference plane so that all heights can be related to either the floor or the level, flat top of a table or chair. Breadths across the body (shoulders, hips, head) can be referred to an implied medial plane of symmetry. But in only a few cases were depth dimensions related to a definable coronal plane (see Figure 4, page 22, for coronal plane orientation). In the future, anthropometrists must concentrate on better definition of "depth" dimensions in terms of starting or stopping points relative to common anterior-posterior locations, and they must measure more depths and breadths of arms, legs, feet, and so on. (Note that anterior-posterior and medial reference planes are not necessarily located in the center of the limbs.)

Accuracy sufficient for engineering purposes often can be achieved with simple scales or grid markings on a wall, floor, or table and rectangular blocks of wood or other rigid material to bridge the gap between the body and the reference plane. Figure 6 illustrates one setup that has been successfully used in surveys in which complex, detailed measurements were not necessary. Note that the two grid-marked planes make it possible to locate points in two dimensions immediately and directly when the measurer holds a simple block of wood or other firm material with appropriate right angle corners. If the block also has a scale oriented perpendicular to the base that is held against the background board, the measurer can read three coordinates with a single setting.

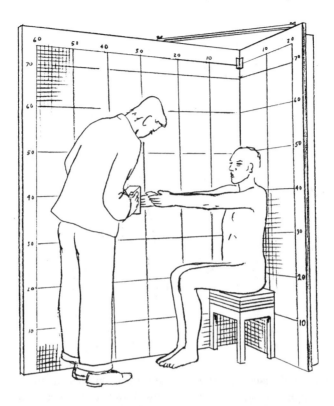

Figure 6. A simple grid board and blocks (Roebuck et al., 1975).

Although the setup illustrated in Figure 6 is not very expensive and is portable, field anthropologists in the past demanded a higher degree of convenience and minimum bulk for transportation. A set of much more compact and readily packaged mechanical devices for use in the field includes the anthropometer, a variety of special spreading and sliding calipers, and flexible tape. Figure 7 illustrates several typical instruments. Adaptable for measuring many parts of the body, nevertheless these finely machined and accurate instruments generally do not permit the simultaneous measurement of landmarks in three dimensions. The anthropometer is basically a rod (that may be separable into sections as shown in Figure 7 as A and D) with one or more sets of scale markings, plus one or more secondary scales (called *branches* or *blades*) mounted at right angles on fittings that slide along the primary rod. The branch attachments also permit sliding adjustments perpendicular to the basic rod. Branches may be straight or curved. When two branches are used together they form a large sliding caliper. Most instruments are marked in metric units, such as millimeters and centimeters.

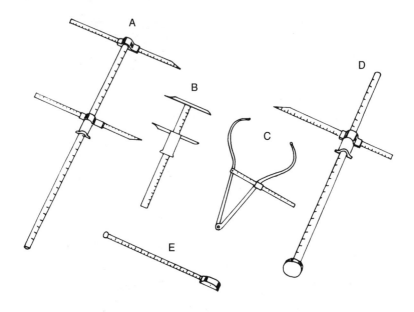

*Figure 7. Typical anthropometric instruments for field use
(courtesy of Kroemer, Kroemer, and Kroemer-Elbert, 1986).*

Figure 8 illustrates typical use of the anthropometer with one branch to measure height from a floor. Figure 9 shows how two branches are used with the main rod to form a large caliper.

Figure 10 shows how a small sliding compass (B in Figure 7) is used for Hand Breadth measurement. Another type of instrument, called a *spreading caliper* (C in Figure 7), has curved arms that are pivoted in the center. This type of device is sometimes useful for measurements when it is necessary to reach around protrusions on the head. Larger devices of similar shape may be used for measuring Chest Depth at the medial plane and at nipple level. Several models of spreading caliper that are minor variations of the curved-arm design have been devised and used by early researchers, including Broca, Hrdlicka, and Bertillon (Roebuck et al., 1975).

Most applications of these anthropological instruments use one of two techniques: (1) bringing the surfaces of the branches into a light touch or sliding contact with the skin, such as in Bideltoid Breadth measurements (see Appendix B for an illustration), or (2) using a firm pressure against the flesh where there is an underlying bony protuberance, such as in Elbow Breadth (Bone). Extensive training is required to learn how to locate the points of measurement properly, especially those determined by palpation (feeling with the fingers).

Further details of methods for the use of anthropometric instruments are presented in commercially available publications (for example, Lohman et al., 1988) and in several reports that describe plans for or results of military anthropometric surveys (e.g., Clauser et al., 1987; Gordon et al., 1989a, 1989b; Hertzberg et al., 1954). Reports by U.S. military services are usually available at a moderate cost through the National Technical Information Service (NTIS) or without cost through personal contact with persons who prepare such reports in government agencies.

Because of the small market for them, only a few sources sell traditional types of instruments such as anthropometers and calipers (e.g., Seritex, Inc., 450 Barrell Ave., Carlstadt, NJ 07072). Special devices are almost universally homemade — that is, fabricated by the user as needed in the development shops of manufacturing companies, a local cabinet shop, or even the researcher's garage or basement.

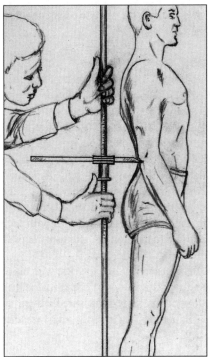

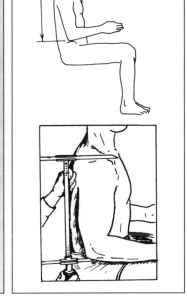

Figure 8. Typical use of an anthropometer for the measurement of height (Roebuck et al., 1975, after Hertzberg et al., 1954).

Figure 9. Use of an anthropometer as a large sliding caliper for measuring Shoulder-Elbow Length (Roebuck et al., 1975, after Hertzberg et al., 1954).

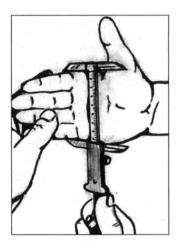

Figure 10. Use of the small sliding compass for measuring Hand Breadth (after Hertzberg et al., 1954).

Circumferences and Arcs

Direct-contact measurement of distances along surfaces of the body, such as circumferences and arcs, is typically made with a flexible tape, as is done by most tailors and seamstresses. Other devices, such as rollers that count the number of rotations of a wheel, are seldom used on the yielding surfaces of human skin. However, if castings of body surfaces are made (see below for a discussion of contour measurement), these devices might prove acceptable for measurement of the cast surface. Considerable training and practice are required to learn a consistent technique for applying tension when using the tape.

Skinfold Thicknesses

The measurement of thickness of folds of skin at various sites on the body may be necessary to determine fat content, which is often relevant in estimations of body density, strength, flexibility, and other characteristics, such as somatotypes (see the Glossary). Skinfold thicknesses usually are not of direct value in the design of most work sites or clothing, but they are potentially useful in characterizing various body features that may be helpful in designing clothing, shaping drafting manikins, or developing computer-generated models. Although skinfold measurements seem rather indirect and imprecise as compared with measurements of diameters and circumferences, evidence indicates some useful correlations of skinfold measures with such dimensions as waist circumferences, arm circumferences, and trunk depths, which are of interest for computer modeling.

To make skinfold measurements, the measurer grasps the skin with his or her fingers and pulls it outward into a fold. The thickness of the fold is then determined with a special type of caliper that exerts a measured amount of pressure. Further information on typical methods and sites for such measurements is available in Lohman et al. (1988).

Angles

Measurements of angles are rarely included in large-scale anthropometric surveys and will not be discussed in detail here. However, measurements of angles provide data of value to ergonomics evaluations, especially in studies of comfort and biomechanics. Angles are also sometimes measured to define special shape relationships and are important in the design of computer-generated models and in evaluations of mobility, reach, clearance, and vision. In order to determine posture and the range of joint motion, angles are usually measured with instruments called *goniometers*. Roebuck et al. (1975) and Norkin and White (1985) summarize many of the common manual methods.

Measuring and Recording Size, Shape, and Angles with Special Devices and Procedures

Jigs and Gauges

Figure 11 shows an example of a box-shaped device for the measurement of feet. A grid scale is marked on the horizontal surface. The foot is placed with one side and the back of the heel against the vertical surfaces, then an outline or key points are marked with a vertically oriented stylus or read from a scale with the aid of a right-angle block held against the other surfaces of the foot.

Figure 12 illustrates two other special measurement devices. On the right is a device for measuring the diameters of fingers. Fingers are generally not truly circular in cross section, so this device gives results that may differ from those obtained when the diameters are measured in depth and breadth with a small sliding compass. On the left side is a conical shape for measuring the inside diameter of finger and thumb grasp. The tips of the thumb and selected finger are brought together around the top of the device, then lowered until they can go no farther without separating the tips.

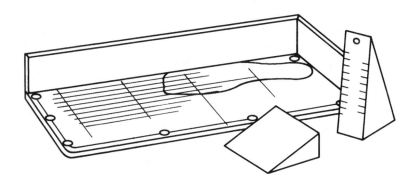

Figure 11. Device for measuring feet (Roebuck et al., 1975, after Hertzberg et al., 1954).

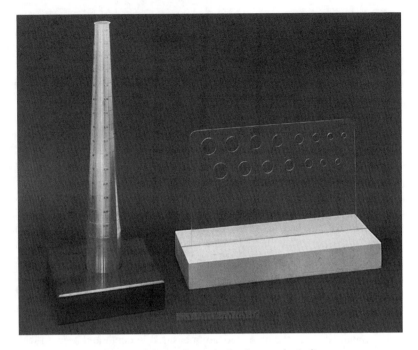

*Figure12. Special devices for measuring finger and grip diameters
(courtesy of Space Division, Rockwell International Corporation).*

Rod Sets for Measuring Contours

Traditional anthropometry has been largely limited to location of a few points or planes on the human body, or to distances between them. The ultimate goal of future anthropometric measurement systems may well be to capture an extensive set of contours of each body in each posture measured. Although this goal has rarely been met, especially with manual, direct-contact methods, some techniques come close to it. For example, devices with multiple, closely spaced probe rods may be used to sample surface contour points in three dimensions, as shown in Figure 13.

Another type of measurement made with contour rods involves locations of points in space that can be reached or that are required for clearance to allow movement of body parts. Figure 14 depicts an example of a device intended to measure reach from a seated position and a defined posture common to older military ejection seats (Kennedy, 1964). In practice, each subject sits in the mockup seat and pushes each of the rods to the maximum limit of reach. The seat is then rotated around a vertical axis, the rods are pushed in by a technician, and the subject repeats the reaching activity. Such a device could also be adapted for measurement of envelopes of space needed for head, elbow, or knee motion, or overall motions of complex activities.

In the future, contact anthropometry methods should focus on more extensive use of mechanical probe devices that register landmark locations in 3D Cartesian or polar coordinates. As compared with traditional anthropometric measurements, data from such measurements are more useful for all work site evaluations and for creating 3D computer-generated models.

Note that although the positions of the rods constitute a record, until the positions are converted to numerical distances on a data document or electronic record, many scientists would say that "measurements" have not been made. Data are frequently summarized as contour lines on a series of planes through the vertical axis. These contours provide data for developing surfaces of reach envelopes or body shapes. There is an important mental and practical distinction between the steps that relate to recording images (whether by contour rods, as described above, or by casting methods, photography, lasers, X rays, or sonic methods, to be described later) and those involving subsequent measurements. Unless the space coordinates, contours, solids, or images produced are converted to digital descriptions, they are not readily subject to mathematical analysis by manual methods or by computer.

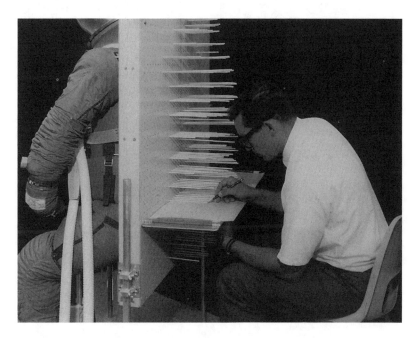

Figure 13. Example of a multiple probe device for making contour measurements (courtesy of Space Division, Rockwell International Corporation).

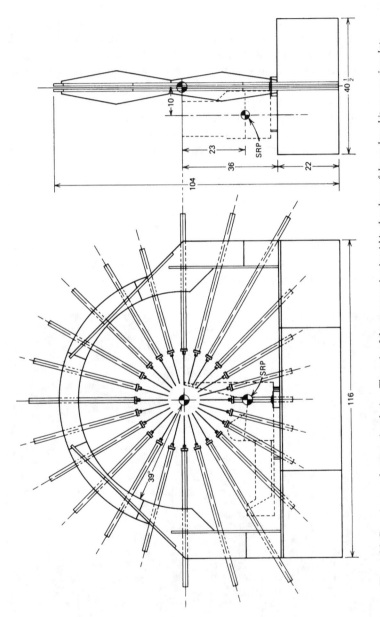

Figure 14. Grasping-reach measuring device. The axis of the seat rotation is within the plane of the arch and its measuring slats (Kennedy, 1964).

36

Although surfaces and curved images may have very fine detail, decisions on how much to measure are crucial because the larger the number of measurements, the greater the effort required in data entry and analysis. Past manual methods dictated that only a few points be measured to ensure that the analysis be manageable within practical time and cost constraints. Future electronic measurement and computer analysis methods will greatly increase the number that are practical, but management of data may always be a serious concern.

Casting

Casting methods are sometimes used for recording fine details of contours in a permanent, three-dimensional form. These may include use of time-honored plaster of paris, modern dental casting materials, or plastics that set at room temperature. Once a permanent record has been made by casting, selected points on defined planes may be measured (perhaps using the previously described multiple rod types of devices) and then analyzed quantitatively with geometrical mathematics and statistics. Records that are made by casting can be analyzed for many potential purposes, including the determination of volumes, areas, mass properties, and various applications involving personal equipment, prostheses, medical evaluations, and forensics. In some practical applications (such as making rubber gloves), there is no need to digitize or analyze the forms produced by casts because the parts to be manufactured may be made directly from a casting without the need for intermediate measurements of the contour or of engineering drawings.

Measuring and Recording Size, Shape, and Angles with Electronic Instruments

In recent years, several direct-contact measurement devices (such as those in Figures 10, 13, and 14) have been provided with electronic readouts that can input digital data directly into computers for instant checking and statistical analysis. In one application, a resistance coil was simply glued to the side of a small sliding compass (Buchholz, 1989). A voltage measurement was then obtained using an electrical contact that moved along the coil as the branch of the compass was adjusted in location.

More sophisticated (and expensive) linear measurement devices are available from manufacturers of specialty measuring equipment (Mitutoyo, 1992). In a few cases, devices have been ganged together in a measuring chair system that can obtain readouts on several standard sitting dimensions for each subject in a shorter time than using individual instruments serially. Electronics have also been incorporated into several types of goniometers (Penny and Giles, 1991; Roebuck et al., 1975).

Electromechanical Probes

Another type of probe device that is gaining popularity consists of an arm with multiple joints that permits its end effector to be placed in a fairly large volume and oriented in different directions with great precision. Sensors at the joints measure the amount of motion used in positioning the end effector and calculate its end location in 3D coordinates (Raab, Fraser, Muhlhan, Hochstadt, and LaCoursiere, 1991).

Sonic Digitization

An alternative method of measuring points in three-dimensional space is for a measurer to use a probe on which are mounted several sound sources, each of which touches a point of interest on the body surface. Records of the sonic signals are then used to determine the end position of the probe in three dimensions. The sound sources are usually electric sparkers whose sonic outputs are sensed by microphones and associated timers. From the difference in time of arrival of signals at each microphone, microcomputers can be used to compute a location for the point of the probe.

Indirect Methods for Measuring Size, Shape, and Angles

Modern technology has made available methods that record electromagnetic waves or sound waves reflected or emanating from the body. Here are a few examples.

Photography and Video Imaging

Various forms of photography and video single-frame imaging are among the most commonplace and well known of the modern indirect methods. For anthropometry, careful definitions of the camera position and orientation are required. To record and extract useful numerical information about the subject's size and shape, use is often made of a number of measurement scales, grids, or markers in 3D space placed around the subject.

One common practice is to place a vertical plate marked with two-dimensional grid lines behind the subject (Li, Hwang, and Wang, 1990). However, such a method can lead to major errors of parallax, as shown in Figure 15. To avoid parallax errors, either more camera locations are required or other markers must be placed at known locations within the field of view. However, if the subject and camera location are known, trigonometric calculations can be used to correct for much of the parallax error (Roebuck et al., 1975). This method was used as recently as 1989 by Li et al. (1990) using special computer software to calculate the corrections.

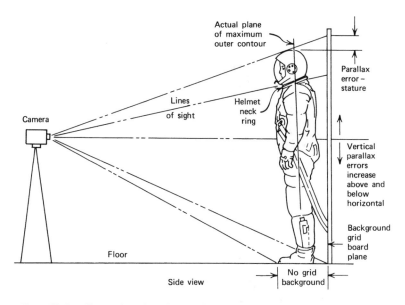

Figure 15. Parallax resulting from the use of a single camera and background grid board (Roebuck et al., 1975).

A lower-technology approach for reducing parallax of grid markings is shown in Figure 16. Although more elaborate than the background grid, it is less complex than computer software. The purpose of this system is to locate the scale indicators in the same plane as the maximum diameters of the subject's body. The parallax errors are generally much reduced in magnitude by this simple practice, especially for body parts that are near the plane of the grid frame (Roebuck et al., 1975). When the subject is in a sitting posture or has limbs in nonplanar orientations, multiple grid frames are needed, and other camera viewpoints may also be desirable.

For localized parts of the body, you may want to develop special jigs, fixtures, and camera combinations that provide controlled body positioning for anthropometric purposes (Roebuck et al., 1975; Zehner, Deason, Ervin, and Gordon, 1987).

Stereo Photography

Simultaneous use of two or more cameras is another way to triangulate on the subject's landmarks in three dimensions. This is the basis for stereo photography that has been used by aerial surveyors to develop contour maps of the earth. The same fundamental process has been used to map contours of faces, hands, and whole human bodies (Burke and Beard, 1967; Herron, 1972, 1973; McConville, Churchill, Kaleps, Clauser, and Cuzzi, 1980;

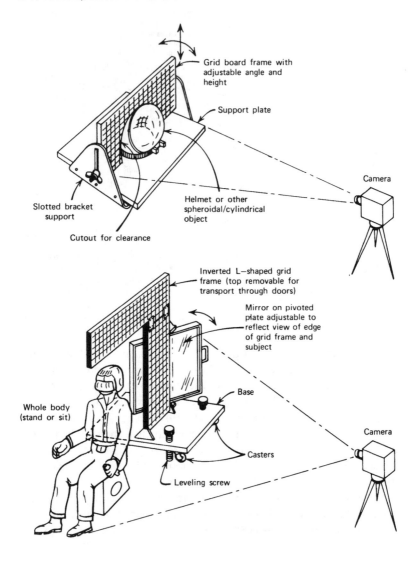

Figure 16. A system of grid board frames to reduce parallax in the photographic recording of contours (Roebuck et al., 1975).

Young et al., 1983). However, the process is neither cheap nor simple: As indicated in Figure 17, several complex steps are required.

One possible method of illustrating the data resulting from stereo photography is in the form of contour maps, as I will describe in Chapter 4. Unfortunately, the data often lack accuracy (Zehner, 1986), although the contours are potentially useful for many purposes. Dimensions measured from stereo photos (or any other photos) do not account for compressing flesh against underlying bone, as can be done with manual application of anthropometers and calipers.

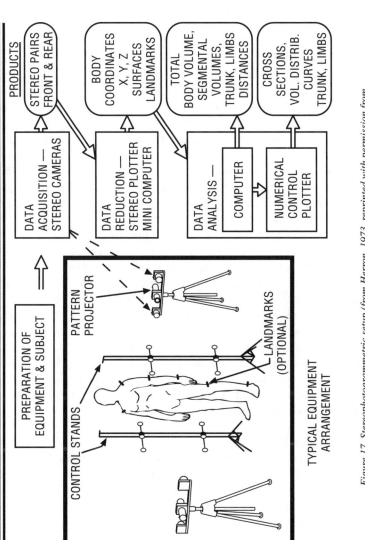

Figure 17. Stereophotogrammetric setup (from Herron, 1973, reprinted with permission from American Association of Physical Anthropologists).

Other problems with this technique include unsatisfactory digitizing schemes and the typical practice of locating contours at standard length increments of distance. For example, McConville et al. (1980) recorded data for cross-sections parallel to the floor on standing subjects. Cross-sections were set at intervals of 2.54 cm (1.0 in) except for the head, hands, and feet, for which the interval was 1.27 cm. The distance between two points around cross-section perimeters ranged from 0.1 to 1.2 cm, with an average of 0.7 cm, apparently without locating them in planes oriented longitudinally with respect to body segments.

Other studies have gathered stereophotogrammetric data on women (Young et al., 1983) and on men in which the cross-sections were spaced at intervals of 2 cm from the floor or other reference plane outside the body. Rather than continue this practice, future stereometric measurements should be based on locations of cross-sections defined to be specific percentages of the distance between joint locations or between landmarks near joints. Also, the number of points around the perimeter of each cross-section should be the same for each cross-section and standardized to lie in planes passing through the link or other central axis in each segment, preferably at equal angular increments. Such approaches would save enormous amounts of time for the interpolation that must be performed on the currently available data in order to express the results in a way that facilitates statistical analyses and modeling.

Some studies have used cadaver material to establish comparisons between direct measurements of physical properties, such as mass and density, and measurements of volume using stereophotogrammetry, anthropometers, and calipers (Chandler, Clauser, McConville, Reynolds, and Young, 1975; Clauser, McConville, and Young, 1969). McConville et al. (1980) measured 31 living male subjects using both stereophotogrammetric and anthropometric techniques, again for the purpose of estimating mass properties.

Although stereophotometric methods have some drawbacks, until recently they represented the most advanced technology for obtaining contour maps of human body parts and enabled 3D data to be described in a common coordinate system.

Stereo Video Recording

What has been done with film and lenses can also be accomplished with video cameras. However, instead of merely inspecting images visually and recording apparent heights, the goal is often to identify pixels of electronic images in two different views that have common characteristics and then calculate their location in 3D space. A process for doing this type of contour definition has been under development in U.S. Navy laboratories for some years, but it is not yet widely used.

Lasers and Other Optical Surface Scanning Methods

Lasers, an acronym for "light amplification by stimulated emission of radiation," are the basis of some of the most promising indirect, high-technology measurement systems for modern anthropometry. Instead of producing an image by gathering externally produced light reflected from an object, laser systems emit extremely narrow beams of specially amplified light and detect the time it takes the beams to return. They can thus provide both distance and position data relative to a two-dimensional plane. Furthermore, all the data are in electronic form and can be directly digitized and interpreted by computers with appropriate software. Currently, the software needed to deal effectively with the large amount of data collected with laser techniques is neither widely available nor capable. However, it is likely that more and better software will be available in a relatively short time, given that the technique seems promising and potentially useful for many imaging purposes.

Laser methods have certain drawbacks and limitations, which they share with cameras: They cannot see obscured armpits or spaces between legs or fingers or behind ears. Another drawback of current laser methods is that they are generally slower than cameras in capturing an image, though much faster than manual methods. This means that the human subject must not move while recordings are being made. As with early portrait photography, subjects need to be given special instructions, and precautions must be taken to avoid blurring and distortion of the image.

Current laser systems lose accuracy when they attempt to measure large objects, such as a whole human body, in one sweep of the camera and light system. Multiple setups and exposures are required. The U.S. Air Force and other agencies are sponsoring development of rapid, whole-body scanning systems, and it seems likely that major improvements in the speed and size of scanned images will be made in the next decade. Even with current limitations, the accuracy possible is as good as or better than stereo photography and certainly more comprehensive than the methods that use manual rods or anthropometers.

Perhaps the most critical consideration in the use of lasers is the high cost of the system, including equipment, software, and computers. That cost looks quite large as a capital investment for a small consulting firm or even a human factors group in a large industry with a moderate budget. A possible lower-cost alternative is to contract out the imaging operations to a company that specializes in such work.

For introductory information comparing laser-based systems, refer to an article by Zehner (1986) that reports on five systems examined for the U.S. Air Force to determine if they are applicable for gathering data on human subjects. The proceedings of a recent workshop on whole-body imaging (Vannier, Yates, and Whitestone, 1993) is another useful source of information.

One of the most widely used, commercially produced laser systems is a software-controlled electromechanical unit that shines a low-intensity laser on an object to digitize its surface in terms of electrical signals (Cyberware, 1990). A high-quality video sensor captures a profile from two viewpoints. Several different setups are possible. However, for measurements of head shapes and other similar objects, the digitizing device is generally mounted on an accurately machined pivoting mechanism or track that moves in small increments around a 3D object to obtain profiles covering the entire visible surface.

One video sensor in the Cyberware system digitizes thousands of profiles in a few seconds to capture the shape of the entire object. A second sensor in the unit simultaneously acquires color information. The scanning process captures an array of digitized points, with each point represented by x, y, and z coordinates for shape and 24-bit RGB (red, green, blue) coordinates for color. Shape and color data are then transferred via an Ethernet link to a graphics workstation for immediate viewing and modification. The screen image may appear in full color as well as correct shape, or it may be defined in terms of contour lines along the surface.

Software available from Cyberware allows the user to manipulate and analyze data in a variety of ways. You can automatically measure attributes such as area and volume, or edit models with operations such as clipping, scaling, and image cutting and pasting. Using software, you can also convert these signals into controlling commands for a machine-carving system to produce a 3D object, such as a bust of a hand or foot. (See multiple-media methods, discussed on page 93.)

A variety of equipment arrangements are also available for specialized areas of the body, such as hands and feet. Techniques have been devised for whole-body imaging with lasers, but these either require lower resolution for a rapid scan or multiple imaging sessions of different body parts in sequence, with the segments to be pieced together later.

Another type of laser system, developed by Marc Rioux at the National Research Council of Canada, ties mobile sending and receiving units together (Rioux, 1989). The obvious alternative to moving the scanning head around the subject is to rotate the subject and keep the scanner fixed in space. This method has been used at the Department of Medical Physics and Bioengineering of the University College London, England (Moss, Coombes, Linney, and Campos, 1991; Moss, Linney, Grinrod, Arridge, and Clifton, 1987). Figure 18 is a schematic illustration of the arrangement. Zehner noted that, in addition to laser systems, there were "recent advances in converting Moiré and raster scan photographic techniques to numeric format" (1986, p. 206). These and other nonlaser systems are described in the proceedings of the workshop on electronic imaging of the whole human body (Vannier et al., 1993).

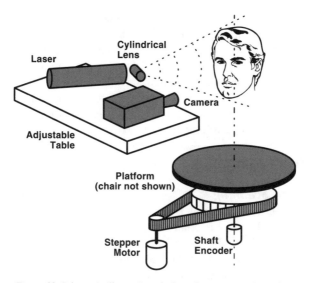

Figure 18. Schematic illustration of a laser beam system for making face contour measurements (Moss et al., 1991).

Phase-Measuring Profilometry System

Other forms of structured light sensing have also been developed for scanning human forms. One of these is called phase-measuring profilometry, or PMP (Halioua, Liu, Bowins, and Shih, 1992; Halioua, Liu, Chin, and Bowins, 1990). Figure 19 illustrates the essential elements of the arrangement.

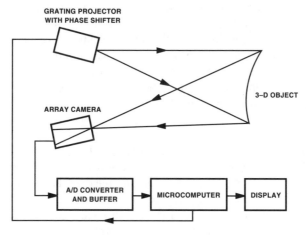

Figure 19. Block diagram of PMP sensing system (Halioua et al., 1992; reprinted with permission).

Only one camera is shown, but in practice, several may be used for different angles. In one arrangement, six cameras are arranged around a fixed subject, and special "structured" light is projected onto the surfaces of the face or body part. Using information about the type of grating through which the light shines and the camera location, software determines the location of points on the surface and creates a set of x, y, z coordinates for these points. There are no moving parts, so a significant advantage of this method is the rapidity with which data are captured.

Internal Imaging

Ultrasonic Scanning

Although ultrasonic imaging is currently in wide use in the medical diagnosis of the condition of internal organs, it is not widely used in anthropometry. Among the problems yet to be resolved are the fuzzy boundaries between different tissues and uncertainties about the accuracy of dimensions in the images. Other problems include the system's relatively high cost and lack of portability. However, future improvements may lead to the broader use of ultrasonic scanning, especially when it is important to locate bone structures and internal organs.

Magnetic Resonance Imaging

Magnetic resonance imaging (MRI), another interesting type of system for internal imaging, has been developed and used in medical practice as a substitute for x-ray photography. MRI scanning has been used at Wright-Patterson Air Force Base in conjunction with laser scanning as part of a study of helmets and head configurations (K. M. Robinette, personal communication, 1993). It is currently limited by the number of different postures that can be accommodated within the machines, which makes whole-body scanning in the seated posture, for example, impossible. MRI scanning also could be enhanced for anthropometric applications if scales and grids of known dimensions were placed in the imaging region.

X Rays

Although x-ray imaging has been used for decades, it is not often employed for measuring living persons, partly because of the hazards of ionizing radiation. Another limiting factor is the relatively high cost of equipment. However, some useful measurements have been made of large numbers of subjects on small portions of the body, such as the hands (Vicinus, 1962), and on small numbers of subjects for locating joints. X rays have also been used on cadavers in a variety of studies.

The parallax problems encountered in photography also apply to x-ray measurements, even though the energy source is on one side of the body and the exposed film on the other. Several computer-aiding methods have been developed to enhance imaging and to selectively image internal planes of the body. It would seem that incorporating a grid frame in the x-ray imaging system could save much of the labor of data reduction and could offer reliable estimates of dimensions of the resulting images. However, I have not seen such methods in use to date.

Methods of Measuring Mass Properties

Engineering design and analysis sometimes require the definition of weight, moment of inertia, location of center of mass, and radius of gyration of body parts and of the whole human body. The quantities in question are known by terms such as *mass properties* or *inertial properties*. (Note that *center of mass*, or CM, is also called *center of gravity*, or CG, in much of the engineering literature.) Data may be needed for the design of dynamic impact test dummies or computer models that check the balance of different postures. Many other engineering and medical evaluations also call for data on mass properties.

Total weight measurement in the clinical environment is a familiar procedure, requiring only that a certifiably accurate scale be obtained for the procedure. Determining the horizontal location of center of mass of the whole body along any given axis can be done with only two scales and a simple platform, as shown in Figure 20 (Roebuck et al., 1975). First, you must determine the center of mass and weight of the platform, then perform a bit of analysis to account for its effects on the total.

The symbols for dimensions and loads in Figure 20 have the following meanings:

$\bar{y}$ = horizontal location of the center of mass measured from the soles of the feet

$\bar{y}_2$ = horizontal location of the center of mass measured from the support point of Scale 2, located near the feet

d = location of the center of mass of the platform (board) measured from the support point of Scale 2

l = horizontal distance between the support points for Scales 1 and 2

W_1 = weight registered on Scale 1 (a portion of the total weight of the person and the weight of the platform supported on the two scales)

W_2 = weight registered on Scale 2 (the remaining portion of the total weight of the person and the weight of the platform supported on the two scales)

W_m = weight of the subject lying on the platform acting at its CM
W_b = weight of the board (platform) acting at its CM
a = distance from the soles of the feet and the support point for Scale 2.

Then

$$W_m = W_1 + W_2 - W_b \qquad (3\text{-}1)$$

and

$$\bar{y}_2 = (W_1 l - W_b d) / W_m \qquad (3\text{-}2)$$
$$\bar{y} = a + (W_1 l - W_b d) / W_m . \qquad (3\text{-}3)$$

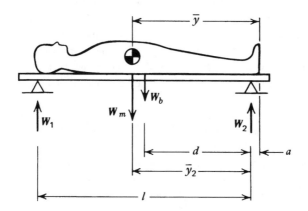

Figure 20. Two-scale method for locating center of mass (Roebuck et al., 1975).

If determination along two horizontal axes (usually orthogonal to each other) is required, the process can be adapted by using two more scales that are located at the sides of a sufficiently wide platform. Only two of the scales opposite each other are used at one time; the others must be lowered or removed so that they do not support the platform. A more complex, balanced platform has been used by the Federal Aviation Administration (Swearingen, 1953; also shown in Roebuck et al., 1975). However, it is not clear whether the complexity of such a device is worth the extra cost of development and resultant time savings.

A variation of the two-scale method involves replacing one scale by a simple fulcrum. The method, described by Reynolds and Lovett (1909), consists of equating the moments around the fulcrum and solving for the unknown distance x. For this solution, you must know the weight of the subject.

Another method of determining the horizontal location of the CM is by suspending the person in a type of chair or framework. This will work for the horizontal location of a single posture, but it is not accurate for simultaneously measuring both vertical and horizontal locations. For example, Chaffee (1961) used this method to determine the horizontal and vertical change of CM location caused by differing angles of accelogravitational forces on ejection seats. By measuring the CM for the seat alone, Chaffee could remove the effect of the seat from the combined measurement for the subject and seat CM to determine the location for the subject alone.

Chaffee's arrangement is shown in Figure 21. His hypothesis was that the vertical location of the CM would be near the center of triangles formed by each set of three successive lines passing through the CM of the suspended seat as it is incrementally tilted either 5 degrees or 10 degrees. Unfortunately, his method yielded strange results (Roebuck, 1976). Chaffee interpreted his data as showing that the CM moves forward (away from the seat back) as well as upward (away from the seat pan) as the seat is incrementally tilted from near upright to near supine angles for the subject. Such a condition is physically impossible because some of the fluids must shift out of the legs and back into the upper trunk, head, and limbs as the backward tilt angle increases. By laying out the geometry of a hypothetical case of such expected CM movement, you can show that, indeed, the centers of the triangles will move forward, away from the seat back, though the actual CM moves slightly backward or parallel to the seat back (Roebuck, 1976).

This example highlights an important problem in the measurement of location of center of mass on living human beings: The measurements are subject to the effects of shifts in body fluids. The assumption that all parts are rigid and unvarying in shape for different postures (as they are for most machinery) is not valid for people. Beside the shifts in fluids, there are also changes in density and tissue concentration, such as through tensing of muscles, or bulging of body segments against each other when certain acute joint angles are assumed. That is why measurements of CM and moments of inertia of body parts of cadavers are usually done with the parts frozen (as, for example, was done by Chandler et al., 1975). If different postures of living subjects are used with the methods in Figure 21 to determine vertical CM locations, the results will be highly suspect. Of the many attempts that have been reported in the literature, unfortunately most are probably not very accurate. To measure both the vertical and horizontal locations for a specific posture, it is necessary to use fundamentally different methods for each. For example, the measurement of the horizontal location might be done with the two-scale method and the vertical location might be measured using a pendulum measurement technique.

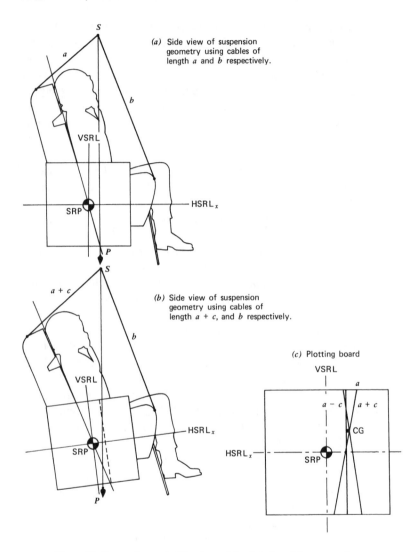

(a) Side view of suspension geometry using cables of length a and b respectively.

(b) Side view of suspension geometry using cables of length a + c, and b respectively.

(c) Plotting board

Figure 21. Suspension method for determining location of the center of mass (from Chaffee, 1961).

The most thorough set of pendulum measurements on living subjects was performed by Santschi, DuBois, and Omoto (1963). This study used an aluminum frame suspended from a high fulcrum, illustrated in Figure 22. The subjects were carefully stabilized in the frame with belts and tape. The pendulum was then given a small push to make it oscillate. From the geometry and period of oscillation, it was possible to determine the location of the height of the center of mass and the moment of inertia of the whole body for a variety of different body sizes. Unfortunately, Santschi et al. did not measure the CM in the horizontal directions using a different technique. Instead, they repositioned the subjects in different orientations on the framework while keeping the same joint angles. Therefore, their horizontal measurements may not correspond correctly with the locations found for the vertical measurements. Researchers take note: Here is a field of anthropometric study that awaits definitive, accurate studies.

Figure 22. The compound pendulum framework for measuring centers of mass (courtesy of Rockwell International Corporation).

As I have mentioned, stereophotogrammetric measurement of living humans and of cadavers can yield contour maps from which you can derive mass properties. The contour maps are used to calculate volume distributions, then assumptions of average density are applied to these volume descriptions to infer the mass properties, such as center of mass and moment of inertia (McConville et al., 1980).

Chapter 4

REPORTING DATA: STATISTICAL SUMMARY METHODS AND PRESENTATIONS

Report Format

Survey reports should include tables of summary statistics, graphics, and text to explain how dimensions were obtained, what instruments were used, and what was the intent of each measurement (what dimension was desired). Thorough reports typically include a photograph and a line drawing to illustrate each measurement. One of the first to use this technique was the report on U.S. Air Force flying personnel measured in 1950 (Hertzberg et al., 1954). Some of these principles of presentation are shown in Figure 23, which consists of two sample pages from a 1989 report (Gordon et al., 1989b).

Other important items that should be included in survey reports include the following:

- Descriptions of methods for marking or finding landmarks
- Descriptions of the methods used to select subjects
- Demographics of the resulting sample: place of birth, racial and ethnic groups, age ranges, classifications by occupation and/or rank, income groups, years of education, gender
- Descriptions of how statistics were calculated
- A glossary of technical terms.

Basic Summary Statistics

Proper analysis and reporting of the results of anthropometric surveys is crucial for future uses of the data. For surveys involving a large number of subjects, the data usually should be summarized in terms of means, standard deviations, and a sufficient number of percentiles to indicate whether the frequency distributions are skewed or kurtotic. Many investigators include specific numerical measures of skewness and kurtosis, measures of confidence, and coefficients of variation (standard deviation divided by the mean).

BYZYGOMATIC BREADTH

The maximum horizontal breadth of the face (between the zygomatic arches) is measured with a spreading caliper.

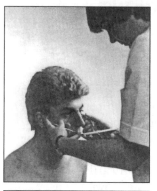

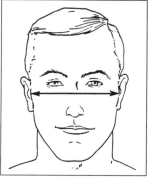

THE PERCENTILES

FEMALES			MALES	
CM	INCHES		CM	INCHES
12.08	4.75	1ST	12.79	5.03
12.17	4.79	2ND	12.95	5.10
12.23	4.82	3RD	13.04	5.14
12.33	4.85	5TH	13.17	5.19
12.49	4.92	10TH	13.36	5.26
12.61	4.96	15TH	13.48	5.31
12.70	5.00	20TH	13.58	5.35
12.78	5.03	25TH	13.66	5.38
12.86	5.06	30TH	13.74	5.41
12.92	5.09	35TH	13.81	5.44
12.99	5.11	40TH	13.88	5.47
13.05	5.14	45TH	13.95	5.49
13.11	5.16	50TH	14.02	5.52
13.18	5.19	55TH	14.09	5.55
13.24	5.21	60TH	14.16	5.58
13.31	5.24	65TH	14.24	5.61
13.38	5.27	70TH	14.32	5.64
13.45	5.30	75TH	14.41	5.67
13.54	5.33	80TH	14.51	5.71
13.64	5.37	85TH	14.63	5.76
13.77	5.42	90TH	14.78	5.82
13.98	5.50	95TH	15.01	5.91
14.12	5.56	97TH	15.15	5.97
14.24	5.61	98TH	15.26	6.01
14.43	5.68	99TH	15.42	6.07

FEMALES		
CM		INCHES
13.13	MEAN VALUE	5.17
.00	SE (MEAN)	.00
.50	STD DEVIATION	.20
.00	SE (STD DEV)	.00
11.70	MINIMUM	4.61
15.00	MAXIMUM	5.91
SYMMETRY—VETA I	=	.26
KURTOSIS—VETA II	=	3.24
COEF. OF VARIATION	=	3.8%
NUMBER OF SUBJECTS	=	2208

MALES		
CM		INCHES
14.05	MEAN VALUE	5.53
.00	SE (MEAN)	.00
.56	STD DEVIATION	.22
.00	SE (STD DEV)	.00
11.80	MINIMUM	4.65
16.10	MAXIMUM	6.34
SYMMETRY—VETA I	=	.18
KURTOSIS—VETA II	=	3.15
COEF. OF VARIATION	=	4.0%
NUMBER OF SUBJECTS	=	1774

Figure 23. Sample pages from a report by Gordon et al. (1989b) showing the use of illustrations and tables to present results.

BYZYGOMATIC BREADTH

FREQUENCY TABLE

	FEMALES					MALES		
F	FPct	CumF	CumFPct	Centimeters	F	FPct	CumF	CumFPct
4	.18	4	.18	11.65–11.75				
4	.18	8	.36	11.75–11.85	1	.06	1	.06
5	.23	13	.59	11.85–11.95	0	.00	1	.06
5	.23	18	.82	11.95–12.05	0	.00	1	.06
18	.82	36	1.63	12.05–12.15	0	.00	1	.06
34	1.54	70	3.17	12.15–12.25	1	.06	2	.11
53	2.40	123	5.57	12.25–12.35	0	.00	2	.11
69	3.13	192	8.70	12.35–12.45	0	.00	2	.11
67	3.03	259	11.73	12.45–12.55	1	.06	3	.17
117	5.30	376	17.03	12.55–12.65	4	.23	7	.39
136	6.16	512	23.19	12.65–12.75	9	.51	16	.90
156	7.07	668	30.25	12.75–12.85	6	.34	22	1.24
141	6.39	809	36.64	12.85–12.95	14	.79	36	2.03
180	8.15	989	44.79	12.95–13.05	11	.62	47	2.65
163	7.38	1152	52.17	13.05–13.15	36	2.03	83	4.68
178	8.06	1330	60.24	13.15–13.25	40	2.25	123	6.93
179	8.11	1509	68.34	13.25–13.35	56	3.16	179	10.09
147	6.66	1656	75.00	13.35–13.45	53	2.99	232	13.08
122	5.53	1778	80.53	13.45–13.55	80	4.51	312	17.59
110	4.98	1888	85.51	13.55–13.65	116	6.54	428	24.13
88	3.99	1976	89.49	13.65–13.75	132	7.44	560	31.57
63	2.85	2039	92.35	13.75–13.85	121	6.82	681	38.39
50	2.26	2089	94.61	13.85–13.95	116	6.54	797	44.93
36	1.63	2125	96.24	13.95–14.05	121	6.82	918	51.75
21	.95	2146	97.19	14.05–14.15	121	6.82	1039	58.57
18	.82	2164	98.01	14.15–14.25	123	6.93	1162	65.50
17	.77	2181	98.78	14.25–14.35	111	6.26	1273	71.76
7	.32	2188	99.09	14.35–14.45	95	5.36	1368	77.11
4	.18	2192	99.28	14.45–14.55	79	4.45	1447	81.57
5	.23	2197	99.50	14.55–14.65	66	3.72	1513	85.29
2	.09	2199	99.59	14.65–14.75	72	4.06	1585	89.35
5	.23	2204	99.82	14.75–14.85	51	2.87	1636	92.22
2	.09	2206	99.91	14.85–14.95	30	1.69	1666	93.91
2	.09	2208	100.00	14.95–15.05	33	1.86	1699	95.77
				15.05–15.15	25	1.41	1724	97.18
				15.15–15.25	14	.79	1738	97.97
				15.25–15.35	10	.56	1748	98.53
				15.35–15.45	10	.56	1758	99.10
				15.45–15.55	8	.45	1766	99.55
				15.55–15.65	0	.00	1766	99.55
				15.65–15.75	5	.28	1771	99.83
				15.75–15.85	1	.06	1772	99.89
				15.85–15.95	0	.00	1772	99.89
				15.95–16.05	0	.00	1772	99.89
				16.05–16.15	2	.11	1774	100.00

In addition, some reports have included graphs of frequency versus size, though these are not easy to interpret. I prefer graphs of normal cumulative probability distributions because they facilitate identification of deviations from the normal distribution. (This will be explained further in Chapter 5.)

When there are many participants in an anthropometric survey, it is of great value to applications personnel to report coefficients of correlation among all pairs of dimensions. Frequent uses of such data include estimations involving summing or subtracting dimensions and the development of regression relationships for defining design requirements. Appendix C contains examples of correlation coefficients tabulated for several dimensions.

Unfortunately, most handbooks do not include correlation coefficients, even though they have appeared in original reports based on some of the larger surveys (Cheverud et al., 1990a, 1990b; Clauser et al., 1972) — often in a volume separate from the means, standard deviations, and percentiles. Roebuck et al. (1975) included tables of bivariate correlations from the 1950 survey of male Air Force flying personnel (Hertzberg et al., 1954). Tables of correlation data from several surveys have also been compiled by Churchill, Kitka, and Churchill (1977).

Regression Equations

Other useful types of information in a survey report are bivariate regressions. Typically these include regressions on Stature and Weight and regressions between the major long-bone dimensions (e.g., Buttock-Knee Length vs. Knee Height, Sitting). To support the design of clothing, survey reports often include regressions between circumferences and tailoring measurements (e.g., inseam, sleeve length). Researchers should compile these regressions directly from individual measurements, though close approximations to such results can be calculated from summary statistics if statistical distributions are normal (Gaussian) and coefficients of correlation between pairs of measurements are reported. In Chapter 5, I will describe how coefficients of correlation are used with ratios of standard deviations to determine slopes that relate values of one dimension to values in another dimension.

In general, variations of each body dimension occur in conjunction with more than one other dimension. Therefore, it is appropriate, according to current trends in anthropometry, to extend the concepts involved with bivariate distributions to develop multivariate regression equations that may deal with three, four, or any other number of variables (Harris, 1975; Meindl, Zehner, and Hudson, 1993; Mood, 1950; Zehner, Meindl, and Hudson, 1993). The number of possible combinations of dimensions in a major survey can lead to a huge number of regression equations, many of which may be of doubtful practical value to most users of the data. Standards of what seems reasonable for the majority of applications have not yet been developed. However, tables of selected multivariate regression equations can be practical and very useful when the subject matter of expected applications is known (e.g., clothing design or work space design).

Several major reports for the Air Force have included regressions for which there are two independent variables, Stature and Weight, for all measurements (Churchill and McConville, 1976; Clauser et al., 1972). Other reports go far beyond these limits to include multiple tables of bivariate regression coefficients and of stepwise multiple variate regression formulas (Cheverud et al., 1990c, 1990d). Fortunately, current computer technology and software help to complete such statistical analyses in a timely and cost-effective fashion.

Multivariate analyses are being further developed to describe even more complex patterns of variability within a population. Among the statistical techniques used in such descriptions are *principal component analysis* (PCA) and *boundary description analysis*. Although much more complex mathematically, and difficult to visualize, multivariate approaches are realistic and powerful methods that will become major elements among the standards for future reporting, for analytical descriptions of trends, for estimating missing data, and for developing design criteria (Zehner et al., 1993). Detailed explanations of these techniques are beyond the scope of this book, but students and applications personnel from other fields should at least be aware of their existence and learn to apply them to analyses and advanced applications in work space design, especially for cockpits of military vehicles.

Normalization of Means

For purposes of estimating and forecasting (as I will explain in Chapter 5), it is helpful to provide some indication of patterns of proportions of body dimensions to one another. For example, it is useful to know if Sitting Height and Thumbtip Reach have the same ratio to Stature in two different populations to help make predictions about lengths of smaller components of the upper body and arms, such as Acromial Height, Sitting, or Shoulder-Elbow Length. Anticipating the need for such analyses, it is a good idea to report the mean of each dimension as a ratio of the mean of a major, commonly measured dimension of the same general type. For example, when considering long-bone lengths (e.g., Buttock-Knee Length, Forearm-Hand Length) and heights, a useful and commonly measured dimension is Stature. Pheasant (1986) denoted ratios of means in which the mean of Stature is the denominator by the symbol E_1:

$$E_1 = \frac{\text{Mean of dimension}}{\text{Mean of Stature}} \qquad (4\text{-}1)$$

Other similar ratios can be developed for comparing breadths, depths, and circumferences. To date, few investigators have reported research on these ratios or their use in estimating standard deviations and proportions (Pheasant, 1986; Roebuck, 1991). However, my experience indicates that they are potentially valuable for purposes of estimating means and proportional relationships, and I believe they should be studied and reported more widely.

Kroemer (personal communication, 1993) commented that, in general, for estimation purposes there should be a coefficient of correlation of 0.7 or higher between the selected major, commonly measured dimension and the other dimensions used to form these ratios. Such magnitudes of correlation are highly desirable for meaningful estimations of one dimension relative to another when the estimations are based on linear regressions. Also, reasonably high correlations are necessary when calculating anthropometric indices (e.g., ratio of Stature to the cube root of Weight) and using them as variables in physiological predictions or for estimating circumferences. However, in the limited context of developing useful summaries of relative proportions of the overall population, expressed simply as ratios of population means, high correlations between dimensions are not so clearly necessary.

Normalization of Variability Measures

Based on my recent studies, and as a useful companion to the ratio E_1, I strongly urge you to report another ratio: the standard deviation of each dimension as a ratio of the standard deviation of the same major, commonly measured dimensions that were selected for normalization of means. When the denominator in such a ratio is the standard deviation of Stature, Pheasant (1986) denoted the ratio E_2:

$$E_2 = \frac{\text{Standard deviation of dimension}}{\text{Standard deviation of Stature}} \tag{4-2}$$

If both E_1 and E_2 were reported in the same survey, they could be valuable for estimating the variability of long-bone lengths and heights in other surveys for which some desired dimensions were not measured. They are also helpful for comparing and estimating the variability of similar types of dimensions within the same population. As I will point out in Chapter 5, Equation 4-2 provides a ratio that is especially useful for comparing relative variability of a dimension across different populations. Normalization relative to a major dimension such as Stature yields a measure of relative variability that is less dependent than the coefficient of variation on the selection standards or other screening factors that are characteristic of a specific population. Such normalized ratios tend to be similar among different populations.

As these ratios are applied to other types of dimensions, such as breadths and circumferences, it may be helpful to use subscripts that are easier to remember and to identify with each different type of ratio. For example, you could use E_{ms} in place of E_1, E_{ss} in place of E_2, or E_{mbb} for the ratio of a mean breadth to the mean Bideltoid Breadth.

Index Statistics

Ratios of summary statistics should not be confused with other useful anthropometric statistics such as indices of proportions that are determined for each individual and then summarized as statistics in their own right, with means and standard deviations. The ponderal index, for example, is an index that is sometimes reported among summary statistics:

$$\text{Ponderal Index} = \frac{\text{Height}}{\sqrt[3]{\text{Weight}}} \qquad (4\text{-}3)$$

In order to better serve the needs of computer-generated modeling, estimating and forecasting activities that are desirable for engineering applications, all future anthropometric reports should contain normalizing ratios of summary statistics and indices of bodily proportions, in addition to simple means, standard deviations, coefficients of variation, and correlation coefficients.

Are Summary Statistics Always Appropriate for Reports?

Investigators should not assume that the foregoing general rules are required for all occasions. Many studies of human strength and biomechanics are so costly and time consuming to set up, perform, and analyze that only a small number of subjects (generally in the range of $n = 6\text{--}20$) can be feasibly involved. In such cases, individual measurements on each subject should be reported. Summary statistics, though a convenience to the reader, are unnecessary because you can always compute summary statistics if you have individual measurements. For small samples, summary statistics tend to hide and gloss over any major differences between subjects. Sometimes one subject's data can have a very large effect on the average and standard deviation, leading to erroneous conclusions. Thus, reporting only summary statistics may make it impossible to combine and weight the data properly with the observations of others doing similar studies.

I have experienced frustration when confronted with means, standard deviations, and correlation coefficients instead of a listing of individual results for samples of 6–10 subjects. My answer to the question posed in the heading of this section is a resounding "NO!"

When reporting dimensions of individuals, always make available, in some sort of archival form (preferably electronic), the measurements of each individual, even for very large surveys. For many applications it is desirable to add or subtract measurements to derive nonstandard dimensions. Although usefully accurate derivations can be made using summary statistics for normally distributed data, nonnormal distributions are much less readily combined. Also, questions often arise about which measurements are likely to be normally distributed and which are not. If the data on individuals were available, these new derivations could be performed in a way that would allow one to have much more confidence in the results.

Contour Descriptions

One common method of describing curved surfaces of envelopes in a numerically useful manner is the so-called contour map. Figure 24 shows an example of a map resulting from a study by Burke and Beard (1967) involving facial features.

Each curved line is the trace of a plane that passes through the surface at a different height from some base plane. Similar maps can be prepared for side views or other cutting planes across the body. The method is useful for real skin surfaces and for imaginary surfaces such as the limits of reach or clearance for body movements. Additional examples for a whole body are shown by McConville et al. (1980). Again, reporting of contour data should be related to the needs of the user (see, for example, the discussion about what heights should be measured in Chapter 3, pages 39–42, stereo photography). These data can be analyzed many different ways, with cross-section cuts taken in only one direction or in two or three mutually orthogonal directions.

Reach envelope data can be related to a variety of different centers or axes, not simply those used in measurement (Kennedy, 1964). Standards are also needed in this area.

Defining and Summarizing Mobility

Anthropometry is also concerned with the measurement of and design requirements for human movements. Measurements of the angular range of joint motion can be used in the development of reach envelopes by proce-dures employing mathematical analyses, drafting manikins, or computer human models. As I will describe later, these reach envelopes are surfaces that define limits of volumes within which to locate controls and connectors or other hand-operated equipment so that they are operable by a large number

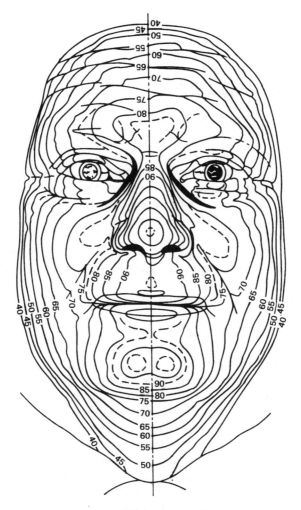

Figure 24. Contour map of the face (Burke and Beard, 1967; reprinted with permission).

of operators. Such surfaces summarize both angular joint motion capability and arm length, plus whatever trunk or leg motions may be involved. They are defined by selected coordinates within 2D and 3D coordinate systems. However, because it is not possible to measure such points for all subjects and for all possible postures, developing envelopes requires knowledge of the angular range of motion of which the human body is capable, as well as the lengths, depths, and breadths of the body parts. Although methods of defining mobility are pertinent to anthropometric methods, they have been omitted in this book because of length constraints.

Chapter 5

FORECASTING AND ESTIMATING

Summary data described in Chapter 4 are absolutely essential for success in anthropometric applications in the same way that building materials are essential for constructing a shopping mall. However, raw building materials are not necessarily ready for such jobs as assembling structures, installing wiring, or attaching gypsum board. First they must be distributed within the job site, cut to appropriate sizes, and mixed or combined with other materials. In anthropometric practice, forecasting and estimating are analogous to the distribution, cutting, and mixing processes in the building trades; they modify and tailor the available body dimension data to make them ready for specific, time-related ergonomic evaluations and engineering design requirements.

Forecasting for All Applications

As defined here, anthropometric forecasting involves determining historical (secular) trends of a few dimensions, usually Stature and Weight, and sometimes trends in proportions. As I explained in Chapter 1, populations are continually changing in their makeup as individuals are added and removed. In addition, many jobs that were once the domain of white males now include females and racial/ethnic minority groups. Construction, piloting, and police work are examples of this type of change.

Because all documented measurement data are from anthropometric surveys conducted in the past, designs for the near or far future should always use predicted data, forecast to an appropriate midpoint or endpoint for the period when the product will be in use. Prediction is especially important for large systems that take a long time from conception to operation (such as the space shuttle) and for those that are to be marketed and in service for many decades. However, because population body dimensions change very slowly, there is little error in using recent survey data for products that will be on the market in a few months and that do not have a long life. In this case, the practical result of prediction may be a decision that any change that has occurred since the latest survey, or that may occur during the life of the product, has no significant effect on design.

Basically, anthropometric forecasting is done by systematically analyzing historical (secular) trends in an attempt to predict changes in Stature, Weight, and other body dimensions. For this reason, it should never be said that old data are useless. When completed, the target dimensions are documented along with the process by which they were derived. Historical analyses of the past century have shown that among many European and American populations, an average increase of about 1 cm per decade in mean Stature has occurred over periods of many decades (Anthropology Research Project staff, 1978a; Greiner and Gordon, 1990, 1992; Jurgens, Aune, and Pieper, 1990; Kroemer et al., 1986; Roebuck, Smith, and Raggio, 1988). However, recent data on British, American, and Norwegian populations suggest that this historical growth has nearly ceased.

In contrast, the Japanese have increased in Stature much faster than have Europeans and are probably still growing. In populations of wide diversity, such as Americans, some ethnic groups may still be rapidly increasing in height, but their effect on the average may be counterbalanced by continued immigration of shorter persons. For further examples of the estimation of trends, see Anthropology Research Project staff (1978a), Chapanis (1975), Greiner and Gordon (1990, 1992), Kroemer et al. (1986), Pheasant (1986), Roebuck (1976), Roebuck et al. (1975), and Roebuck, Smith, and Raggio (1988).

Estimating

In anthropometric estimation, you combine, interpolate, and compare dimensions to derive a few additional dimensions and thus better describe a particular population at a specific point in time, most often to extend the usefulness of data from a published survey. On rare occasions, you may have to combine or otherwise generate a very large number of statistical distributions of dimensions to describe more completely a population about which little of the anthropometry is known (e.g., Lippert, 1965). I prefer to call this kind of massive effort *population synthesis* (Roebuck et al., 1975). The input data for estimation or synthesis may be published summary statistics, individual measurements from one or more surveys, a few forecasted dimensions such as described earlier, or some combination of all of these. The results sought may be dimensions that could have been measured, but were omitted on a particular survey, or dimensions that cannot be measured because the target date of the forecast has not yet occurred. Because estimating missing anthropometric data is a large and complex subject, only some of the basics can be described here. More detailed treatments are available in Pheasant (1986), Roebuck et al. (1975), and related technical articles and reports in the anthropometric literature.

Estimation is often needed because monetary and schedule constraints on anthropometric surveys generally preclude measuring all the dimensions that users desire. Furthermore, new needs often arise after surveys have been completed, and we can expect the same to occur in the future. Computer simulation of human activity is currently one of the activities that demand new data in greater quantities than was common in the past, and it requires more consistent data across populations than has been the case. For example, I recently found that not a single survey among six population surveys of males or any of five surveys of females was able to supply data on all 14 dimensions required for a relatively simple, nongraphical, computer stick-man model called Crewstation Assessment of Reach, Version IV (Roebuck, 1991).

The estimation methods available to help fill the empty data cells are generally of two types: (1) those that are almost purely mathematical/statistical in nature (sometimes called *derived dimensions*) and (2) those that depend at least partly on empirically observed, biological characteristics or constraints. In this book, I call the latter *biometric similarity relationships*. Either may involve a variety of geometrical relationships.

Mathematical/Statistical Estimating Principles

The main mathematical relationships involved in estimation are (1) statistical formulas and algebraic relationships dealing with the variability of measurements within populations and (2) geometric/trigonometric relationships, which relate mainly to individual shapes and proportions, whether or not the results are subject to statistical manipulation. In fact, the distinction between the two is mostly philosophical, given that standard statistical manipulations may be applied to some simple and obvious, anatomically valid geometric concepts, such as adding dimensions of Hand Length and Elbow-Wrist Length to estimate Forearm-Hand Length.

However, trigonometric and geometric principles tend to become the main concern when dealing with triangulation from known landmarks to locate others, or when analyzing angular relationships of body parts to calculate link lengths. Once the basic geometrical relationships have been determined, you can estimate the variability of the distances and angles of the relevant component elements.

Simple Statistical Conversions

Frequently, estimations need deal only with relatively elementary concepts, such as determining the standard deviation for dimensions from the commonly reported data in human factors handbooks. Often such tables list only 5th percentiles, means (which are equal to 50th percentiles for normal distributions), and 95th percentiles. MIL-STD-1472 (U.S. Department of Defense, 1989) lists only 5th and 95th percentiles, but these are not necessarily from the same survey, so any results of conversions must be considered as combined population data of uncertain pedigree. Another example is estimating some other percentiles, say the 98th or the 20th. A third typical question is: Given a subject of a specific size, what percentiles do his or her measurements match in a given population? These types of estimations I call *conversions* of information from one form to another.

Assuming that the measurements in question are normally distributed (or nearly so), alternative expressions can be determined with accuracy by rather simple approaches, using either statistical tables or graphic methods. (Methods for dealing with nonnormal distributions are only briefly mentioned in this book.)

Those who prefer to work with numbers can begin by finding a table of factors to be multiplied by the standard deviation to determine percentiles for normal distributions. Table 1 is an abbreviated example. More extensive tables found in some elementary statistics texts (e.g., Dixon and Massey, 1951, p. 306) typically do not use the term *percentiles*, but instead list areas under the normal curve. These areas are equivalent to decimal fractions of the population and may be converted to percentiles by multiplying the area by 100. It is customary to round downward to the nearest whole digit, but some authors like to use decimal fractions, such as the 2.5th percentile.

TABLE 1
Factors for Computing Percentiles from Standard Deviations

Percentile		K_1	Central Percentage Covered	$K_2 = 2K_1$
30	70	0.524	40	1.045
25	75	0.674	50	1.349
20	80	0.842	60	1.683
15	85	1.036	70	2.073
10	90	1.282	80	2.563
5	95	1.645	90	3.290
2.5	97.5	1.960	95	3.920
1.0	99.0	2.326	98	4.653
0.5	99.5	2.576	99	5.152

Source: Roebuck (1957)

Examples:

1. To find the 95th percentile, use $K_1 = 1.645$. When $\bar{X} = 35.1$ cm and $S = 1.5$ cm,

> *$1.5 \times 1.645 = 2.5$ cm*
> *$35.1 + 2.5 = 37.6$ cm, the 95th percentile.*

2. To find the range needed to accommodate the middle 90% of the same group:

> *$1.5 \times 3.29 = 4.9$ cm, the range of adjustment.*

The normal curve is symmetrical around the mean, so many tables list only the area from the mean out to three standard deviations (about half of the total area). To obtain percentiles using tables of this kind, you must add 0.50 to the values above the mean or subtract values below the mean from 0.50. Also, many tables do not list areas in simple decimal increments (e.g., 0.1, 0.3, 0.45) but, rather, relate the area to simple decimal increments of the number of standard deviations from the mean. Interpolation may be necessary to determine the desired factor(s).

As an example, find the standard deviation of a distribution from the 5th and 95th percentiles. The 5th percentile is below the mean a distance of 1.645 times the standard deviation, and the 95th percentile is above the mean a distance of 1.645 times the standard deviation. The standard deviation may be estimated in one of two ways:

1. Subtract the value for the 5th percentile from the 95th. Divide the difference by 2 × 1.645, or 3.29. The result is the standard deviation.
2. If the mean is provided, subtract the value for the 5th percentile from the mean or subtract the mean from the 95th percentile value. Note that in a normal distribution the mean is halfway between the 5th and 95th percentiles. For normal distributions, the same answer should be found by either subtraction. Divide either difference by 1.645. The result is the standard deviation.

Tabulated values for percentiles may be coarsely rounded, perhaps to only two significant figures (Anthropology Research Project staff, 1978b), so that different approaches may yield slightly different results even if the original data were normally distributed.

For those who like to work with graphic approaches, on a sheet of normal probability graph paper, plot the 5th and 95th percentiles against the anthropometric dimension on the linear scale. Figure 25 provides a sample plot of such points for Hand Length of male Air Force flying personnel, shown with solid circles. Draw a straight line through the two plotted points (solid line in Figure 25). The result is a line that represents the cumulative normal distribution and permits you to graphically estimate any desired percentile value. The open circles on the graph are actual data showing that the distribution is nearly normal — that is, the data lie close to the straight line.

When using this graphical method, it is not necessary to determine the standard deviation to find any specific percentile values. However, the standard deviation can be found, to a close approximation, by subtracting the value for the 16th percentile from the mean value (50th percentile) or subtracting the mean value from that for the 84th percentile. The reverse process can be used to determine percentiles if you are given only means and standard deviations in a table of anthropometric dimensions.

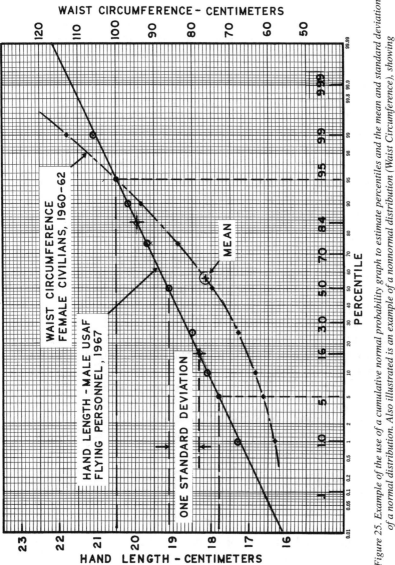

Figure 25. Example of the use of a cumulative normal probability graph to estimate percentiles and the mean and standard deviation of a normal distribution. Also illustrated is an example of a nonnormal distribution (Waist Circumference), showing the typical concave upward form of dimensions involving regions with significant amounts of fatty tissue.

67

If data are given in both metric and English units to the same number of decimal places, as in NASA Reference Publication 1024 (Anthropology Research Project staff, 1978b), a more accurate estimate of the standard deviation (and other percentiles) can be obtained by using the metric data.

Also shown in Figure 25 is a broken line with a concave upward curve connecting solid diamonds. This is an extreme example of a distribution that is not normal, although it can be plotted on the same scale as the normal ones. Such curves are typical for Weight and for circumferences around body volumes composed mostly of soft flesh. Percentiles can still be readily obtained by graphical interpolation, but the use of tabulated factors for normal distributions no longer applies. Accurate estimates of standard deviations are not easily obtainable from such curved lines.

Adding and Subtracting Dimension Distributions

For many applications, you must combine dimensional data by either adding or subtracting known data within a population to obtain a new result. (For combining data of two or more populations, see Pheasant, 1986, or Roebuck et al., 1975.) For example, how would you estimate the 95th percentile Forearm-Hand Length from the two separate distributions of Elbow-Wrist Length and Hand Length? A commonly suggested approach is to add two 95th percentile lengths to obtain an estimate for the 95th percentile of the sum. However, several authors (e.g., Annis and McConville, 1990; Churchill, 1978; Daniels, 1952) have shown that this is incorrect because it does not take into account the correlation between dimensions. The correct procedure is to add the arithmetic means of the two distributions, then determine the standard deviation of the resulting combination, and finally estimate the desired percentile of the new distribution using the calculated standard deviation (Churchill, 1978; Pheasant, 1986; Roebuck et al., 1975).

Estimating Means and Standard Deviations

Expressed algebraically, the necessary equations for adding two distributions are as follows:

$$M_3 = M_1 + M_2 \tag{5-1}$$

$$S_3 = (S_1^2 + S_2^2 + 2r_{12}S_1S_2)^{.5}. \tag{5-2}$$

In these equations, M_1 and M_2 are the means of the first and second variables, respectively (say, Elbow-Wrist Length and Hand Length); M_3 is the mean of the sum (Forearm-Hand Length); S_1 and S_2 are the standard deviations of the first and second variables, respectively; S_3 is the standard deviation of the sum (a third variable); and r_{12} is the coefficient of correlation between Variables 1 and 2.

The top of Figure 26 illustrates the anatomically valid, geometrical relationship between the given and desired dimensions. The given input values for the means, standard deviations, and correlation coefficients are shown in lines 1 and 2 of Figure 26. Note that if the two distributions are each normally distributed, the distribution of their sum also will be normally distributed. The calculated results from Equations 5-1 (mean) and 5-2 (standard deviation) are shown in italics in line 3. Once you have determined the mean and standard deviation of the combination, calculating the 95th percentile is a simple matter of adding the mean to 1.645 times the standard deviation.

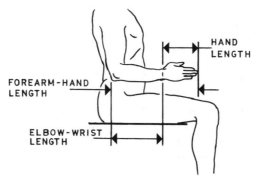

Dimension	Mean	S	Correlation Coefficients		
			1	2	3
1. Hand Length	7.52	0.32		0.643	
2. Elbow-Wrist Length	11.81	0.56	0.643		
3. Forearm-Hand Length	*19.33*	*0.80*			

Figure 26. An illustration of the solution of the following problem: Find the mean and standard deviation of Forearm-Hand Lengths for U.S. Air Force flying personnel given statistical data for Hand Lengths and Elbow-Wrist Lengths including the correlation between them.

Thus,

$$\text{95th percentile} = (1.645 \times S_3) + M_3 \tag{5-3}$$
$$= (1.645 \times 0.80) + 19.33 = 20.65 \text{ in, or}$$
$$= (1.645 \times 2.03) + 49.10 = 52.44 \text{ cm.}$$

A similar set of formulas can be used for subtraction of two known dimensions (Pheasant, 1986; Roebuck et al., 1975):

$$M_3 = M_1 - M_2 \tag{5-4}$$
$$S_3 = (S_1^2 + S_2^2 - 2r_{12}S_1S_2)^{.5}. \tag{5-5}$$

Estimating Coefficients of Correlation

After a mean and a standard deviation of a sum or difference have been
determined, the next question that may arise is how to estimate the coefficient of correlation between the result and each of the two known distributions that were used to produce it. Such correlations are often needed for
advanced methods of generating synthetic populations in human modeling
by computer or for formulating regression equations, such as the regression
of the sum (Forearm-Hand Length) on one of the two addends (say, Elbow-
Wrist Length). The formulas for calculating the correlation coefficients for
the sum are

$$r_{13} = (S_1 + r_{12}S_2)/(S_3) \tag{5-6}$$
$$r_{23} = (S_2 + r_{12}S_1)/(S_3) \tag{5-7}$$

In these formulas, r_{13} is the coefficient of correlation between Variables
1 and 3, r_{23} is the coefficient of correlation between Variables 2 and 3, and
S_1, S_2, and S_3 are the standard deviations of Variables 1, 2, and 3, respectively. Note that S_3 should be calculated using Equation 5-2. In Table 2,
examples of estimated coefficients of correlation are shown in italics using
the input data and results from Figure 26.

TABLE 2
An Illustration of the Solution to the Problem "Estimate the Correlation Coefficients
between (1) Forearm-Hand Length and Hand Length and (2) Forearm-Hand Length and
Elbow-Wrist Length Given Statistics for Hand Length and Elbow-Wrist Length Separately"

| Dimension | Mean | S | Correlation Coefficients | | |
			1	2	3
1. Hand Length	7.52	0.32		0.643	*0.846*
2. Elbow-Wrist Length	11.81	0.56	0.643		*0.952*
3. Forearm-Hand Length	19.33	0.80	*0.846*	*0.952*	

Source: adapted from Roebuck (1989).

Similar formulas are used for calculating the coefficients of correlation
between a calculated difference and the two known dimensions:

$$r_{13} = (S_1 - r_{12}S_2)/(S_3) \tag{5-8}$$
$$r_{23} = (r_{12}S_1 - S_2)/(S_3) \tag{5-9}$$

The definitions of terms in these two equations are generally the same as
for addition, except that S_3 should be calculated from Equation 5-5, as is

appropriate for subtraction of variables. Note carefully the locations of terms and signs in the numerators for these equations; they are not exactly the same as for addition.

Regressions of One Dimension on Another

In many applications of anthropometric data, you may want to know if one body dimension in a population tends to change with another (or with several others). For example, in designing seating adjustments for automobiles, the relationship between leg length and height of the eye from the seat has been used to minimize the complexity of the design of the seat height and fore-aft adjustment. Most introductory textbooks on statistics provide formulas describing such relationships, called *regression equations*. When two sets of measurements are normally distributed, a linear relationship defines the mean value of the dependent $(\hat{Y})$ variable for given values of the independent one (X) — that is,

$$\hat{Y} = a + bX. \tag{5-10}$$

The constant b is the slope of the line defining the relationship between the two variables, and a is the intercept constant — that is, the value of $\hat{Y}$ when $X = 0$. The slope is calculated by the following formula:

$$b_{yx} = (r_{xy})(S_y/S_x) \tag{5-11}$$

where S_y and S_x are, respectively, the standard deviations of the dependent variable and the independent variable, and r_{xy} is the coefficient of correlation between the two variables.

Figure 27 illustrates a bivariate regression relationship of Hand Length on Elbow-Wrist Length for the same population as in the problems relating to Figures 25 and 26. Note that the line on the graph passes through the means of both variables. These means are used to calculate the constant a:

$$a = M_y - b(M_x) \tag{5-12}$$

where M_y is the mean of the dependent variable $(\hat{Y})$ and M_x is the mean of the independent variable (X).

Unlike percentiles and standard deviations, regression equations may be algebraically added or subtracted to yield a valid new regression equation.

For additional details and sample problems, see standard statistical textbooks (e.g., Dixon and Massey, 1951; Harris, 1975; Mood, 1950). The principles illustrated may be extended to multivariate analyses of several varieties (Meindl et al., 1993; Zehner et al., 1993).

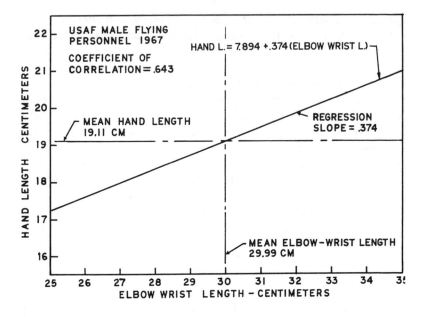

Figure 27. Example of regression graph and equations.

Software

For many statistical calculations, software tools are available for use in personal computers and graphics workstations, minicomputers, and mainframes. Examples of powerful programs for high-end computers are SAS (SAS Institute, Box 8000, Cary, NC 27512-8000), SPSS (SPSS Inc., 444 N. Michigan Ave., Chicago, IL 60611), and BMDP (BMDP Statistical Software, Inc., 1440 Sepulveda Blvd., Suite 316, Los Angeles, CA 90025). In most cases, these can be used or adapted to make the calculations described here. For simpler analyses, spreadsheets and associated graphics programs may suffice.

Biometric Similarity Relationships

In addition to strictly mathematical approaches, patterns of similarity between ratios of means and variabilities across different populations and within certain morphological classifications of human dimensions help in estimating dimensional data that were not measured in a given anthropometric survey. I call these patterns *biometric similarity relationships* because their validity depends on empirically derived human body dimensional relationships based on measurements reported in anthropometric surveys, rather than on purely statistical methods.

Biometric similarity relationships make it possible to estimate factors such as standard deviations of dimensions based on typical proportions and the type of dimension (e.g., long-bone lengths and heights, depths, and breadths of soft tissues or bony tissues, or circumferences of soft tissues or bony portions of the body). Other factors that often need to be established with the use of biometric similarity relationships are racial or ethnic group, gender, age ranges, and occupational or fitness selection requirements. Social or cultural factors are also sometimes significant factors in these estimations.

Following are some general methods for estimating means and standard deviations based on biometric similarity.

Matching Populations

If possible, use summary data on the same body dimension from another population that has nearly the same mean and standard deviation for several other body dimensions that were measured in both surveys — for example, Mid-Shoulder Height, Sitting, measured on Naval aviators in 1964. Their mean Stature was 177.65 cm with a standard deviation of 5.92 cm. It is reasonable to expect that the distribution (mean and standard deviation) of that dimension would be about the same for Air Force flying personnel in 1967, who had a mean Stature of 177.34 cm and standard deviation of 6.19 cm.

The concept of population matching was carried even further by McConville, Robinette, and Churchill (1981), who matched raw data on Stature and Weight of individual civilians with individual military personnel who had similar Statures and Weights. Each of the military individuals had been measured in a much larger number of dimensions than the civilians, and these additional dimensions were assumed to have the same values for the civilians. Summarizing the statistics for the matched individuals gave an estimate of statistics for the population sample for which matches could be found. Though promising as far as it went, there were some extremes of size among civilians for which a good match could not be found in the military population.

Constant Coefficients of Variation

This method for estimating standard deviations is based on the assumption that if selection characteristics for each of two populations are equivalent, the coefficients of variation for each dimension measured can be expected to be equal in the two populations. It is not necessary that the populations have matching means or standard deviations if the ratios of standard deviation to mean show a reasonable match. If the two different populations are designated a and b, then the assumption is that

$$S_a/M_a \;=\; S_b/M_b \quad \text{or} \quad S_a \;=\; S_b \times M_a/M_b, \tag{5-13}$$

where S_a is the standard deviation to be estimated (unknown), S_b is the standard deviation of the same dimension in population b where applicable data were reported (known), M_a is the mean for the dimension in the population to be estimated (must be known to use this method), and M_b is the known (reported) mean in population b.

The ratios S_a/M_a and S_b/M_b are each coefficients of variation, often designated V in statistical parlance, and are expressed as percentages rather than as fractions.

If the selection characteristics are not similar for the two populations being compared, another adjustment ratio using coefficients of variation can be applied using data for two other known dimensions (usually Stature or Weight). For example:

$$S_a = S_b \times M_a/M_b \times V_{as}/V_{bs}, \tag{5-14}$$

where V_{as} is the coefficient of variation for Stature for population a and V_{bs} is the coefficient of variation for Stature for population b. Use of such an adjustment ratio is based on the assumption that general population selection factors for a given population affect all dimensions and will thus tend to increase or decrease variabilities across all dimensions in constant proportion to that of another population.

Ratio Scaling

When the dimensions in the two populations are clearly different (the usual case) but have other apparently similar racial or occupational characteristics, it is reasonable to adjust the predictions for both means and standard deviations in proportion to the actual values of key dimensions, such as Stature, Weight, and Chest Circumference. In Chapter 4, two useful prediction ratios were defined, E_1 and E_2 (Equations 4-1 and 4-2). Pheasant (1986) calls this approach the *method of ratio scaling*.

For example, suppose that the standard deviation for the distribution of Stature is known (or has been estimated) for a selected population (here designated a). Then the standard deviation for another dimension, such as Shoulder-Elbow Length for population a may be estimated from data of another population (here designated b), for which the standard deviation for both Stature and Shoulder-Elbow Length are known. The method uses the ratio E_2 that was defined in Equation 4-2:

$$E_2 = S_b/S_{bs} = S_a/S_{as}, \tag{5-15}$$

where S_a is the standard deviation to be estimated (unknown), S_b is the standard deviation of the same dimension in population b where applicable data were reported (known), S_{as} is the standard deviation of Stature for population a (known), and S_{bs} is the standard deviation of Stature for population b (known). Solving for the unknown standard deviation,

$$S_a = E_2 \times S_{as}. \tag{5-16}$$

Similar approaches may be used involving ratios of standard deviations to body dimensions other than Stature.

Variability Pattern Analysis

Even when you are estimating standard deviations of entirely new, nonstandard dimensions, help is available from a method based on generalizing the foregoing concepts in terms of typical variability pattern analyses. Pheasant (1986) calls this method *empirical estimation of standard deviation.* To obtain the greatest confidence of results, you must know the morphological measurement classification (length, breadth, depth, or circumference) and judge whether the body segment being dimensioned is mostly bone or mostly soft tissue. Although generally less precise than the three foregoing methods, this method offers a ballpark estimate that is often accurate enough for many engineering applications. Furthermore, the process of organizing the data for applying the method provides insights about patterns of human dimensional variability that can be extremely helpful in estimating dimensions within a population and in synthesizing new populations from minimal data.

To apply this method requires substantial research and preparation. For example, suppose you want to estimate the standard deviation for a specific dimension, such as Forearm-Hand Length (a long-bone length) for Air Force flying personnel in 1967, but you have only the mean (49.1 cm = 19.33 in). Because such data are not yet assembled conveniently in the literature, you must first compile data on standard deviations and means of a large number of height and long-bone lengths from a survey of the population of interest or another population that has similar relative variability characteristics. It is very helpful to plot such data as shown in Figure 28, in which each point represents the data for one body dimension.

The mean for a dimension is plotted on the horizontal axis and its corresponding standard deviation is plotted on the vertical axis. In Figure 28, several points are identified by name, together with their associated coordinates, which are shown in parentheses. The slope of a line connecting the origin and the coordinates for each dimension is equal to the coefficient of variation for that dimension. For example, the slope of the dashed line in Figure 28 is equal to the coefficient of variation for Stature. The patterns of points usually have the following characteristics:

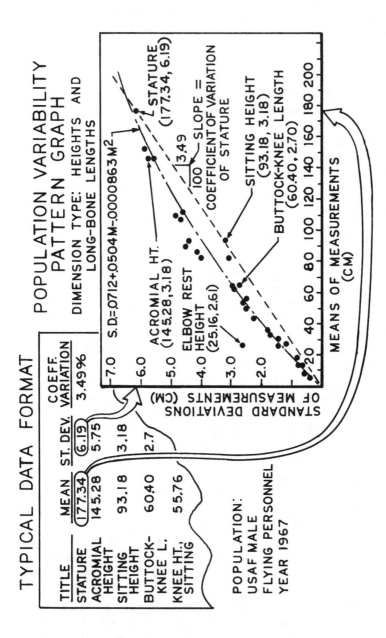

Figure 28. A graph showing the typical trend of increasing magnitude of standard deviation as the mean increases for several heights and long-bone lengths from a single population. Source: Anthropology Research Project Staff (1978b).

1. Because few or no points fall below the dashed line, the coefficients of variation of dimensions in this classification (heights and long-bone lengths) are usually equal to or greater than that of Stature.
2. The point representing Sitting Height nearly always lies very near the dashed line, indicating that Sitting Height has a coefficient of variation nearly the same as that for Stature.
3. The majority of points cluster around an upwardly convex arc (shown by a dot-dash line in Figure 28) that appears to cross the straight dashed line near the origin and near the point representing Stature.

Roebuck (1957, 1991) and Pheasant (1986) have shown that for many populations, such an arc can be described by a nonlinear regression (least squares fitted curve) of the standard deviation on the mean — that is, by a second-order polynomial of the form

$$\hat{S} = a + bM - cM^2, \tag{5-17}$$

where $\hat{S}$ is the expected value of standard deviation for a given mean value of a dimension, M; a is constant; and b and c are coefficients that define the average slope and curvature of the regression. In this example, the equation derived by least squares fit to the data, using units of centimeters for means and standard deviations, is

$$\hat{S} = 0.0712 + 0.0504M - 0.0000863M^2. \tag{5-18}$$

Pheasant (1986) suggested the following formulas as first approximations for adults in Great Britain when the mean (M), in millimeters, is known or can be calculated:

Men: $\hat{S} = 0.05703M - 0.000008347M^2.$ (5-19)
Women: $\hat{S} = 0.05783M - 0.000010647M^2.$ (5-20)

Equations 5-18 through 5-20 are examples of ways to calculate the approximate standard deviation of any long-bone length or height given only the mean of the statistical distribution within a population.

Pheasant (1986) determined the value of coefficient a to be zero in Equations 5-19 and 5-20, and it is usually very small. Actually, the numerical values of coefficients in such empirical relationships are dependent on which specific measurement data are used to derive the equations and on the particular population's variabilities.

For an extreme example, suppose that only two measurements were selected, such as Sitting Height and Stature. In this case, there would be no "curve," only a straight line connecting the two points, and the coefficient of the squared term would appear to be zero. Therefore, when you make comparisons of such curves between two sets of population data, be sure to use the exact same measurements from each population.

Also, do not be misled by how the dimension name was selected by anthropologists in the past. Consider the dimension Elbow Rest Height, whose plotted point is identified in Figure 28. It has a greater standard deviation than the other points with a similar mean value. Although called a height, in fact it is a measure of empty space between the elbow and seat that is not governed by the laws of biological growth in the same manner as most body segments. One could argue that it does not belong to the same family of measurement data as the others (in fact, it was not included in calculating coefficients for Equation 5-18).

Figure 28 suggests that, for dimensions of similar morphological characteristics, standard deviations are roughly proportional to their means. This fact is helpful for estimating within populations. Observations of several of these graphs for different populations has led me to hypothesize that the general shape of such patterns (relating standard deviations of dimensions to means of dimensions for long-bone lengths and heights) is common for all human populations. However, I recognize that the position of each point relative to that for Stature may vary a small amount from one population to another, depending on the typical body proportions. For example, the ratio of Sitting Height to Stature for Japanese is greater than for white, northern Europeans or for Blacks (Damon, Stoudt, and McFarland, 1966).

After searching for a way to analyze and demonstrate the essential similarities among plotted patterns of standard deviations versus means of measurements, I have discovered the following simple method. Divide the mean value for each measurement by the mean for Stature, and divide the standard deviation for each measurement by the standard deviation of Stature. The resulting ratios are, respectively, those denoted E_1 and E_2 by Pheasant (1986), as defined in Chapter 4 (Equations 4-1 and 4-2), used for the method of ratio scaling.

If these transformations were applied to the data that were graphed in Figure 28, the resulting graph would appear exactly the same in regard to the pattern of locations of points relative to each other, but the units of the horizontal scale would be fractions (the ratio E_1) and those of the vertical scale also would be fractions (the ratio E_2), both of which will range from zero to a little over 1.0. On such a graph, the coordinates of Stature are always (1.0,1.0). Or, if the ratios are expressed as percentages (Roebuck et al., 1975), the coordinates of Stature would be (100,100). The horizontal scale can be said to define the average proportion of each dimension relative to Stature. The vertical scale could be called the *Stature-normalized variability*.

When data from several different populations are displayed in this Stature-normalized manner, not only are the patterns similar in appearance, but the numerical coefficients for the formulas of the curves fitted to each set of population data may also be nearly identical. I have demonstrated this remarkable phenomenon for populations as different as males and females in the Air Force (Roebuck, 1991).

Similar approaches can be used for estimating standard deviations of circumferences, depths, and breadths (Pheasant, 1986). For example, for estimating standard deviations of circumference, the key dimension might be Shoulder Circumference or Chest Circumference. I would avoid the use of Waist Circumference or Waist Depth as key dimensions because they typically have high standard deviations whose relationships to other circumferences, depths, and breadths are difficult to predict.

Empirical Geometrical Methods

Estimation of body depth and breadth as a function of circumferences for the same cross-sections is an example of the application of semi-intuitive empirical methods. Because many limb cross-sections are approximately elliptical or circular in shape, dividing the circumferences by pi (3.1416) should yield an approximation of their average diameters. However, the circumference of almost any body cross-section is larger than the circumference of an ellipse of the same breadth and depth. By measuring the circumferences of many body cross-sections on large samples of persons, it is possible to derive empirical formulas, such as regressions or ratios, that relate depths and breadths of given cross-sections to their circumferences. Determination of such factors for the many body cross-sections needed for human modeling is a task requiring much further study.

Other problems of the same nature have to do with the shapes of curvatures for back and limb surfaces, head shapes, joint ranges of motion, link rest postures, and positions of joint centers of rotation. Currently, solutions to these problems depend on data from reports of rare studies involving a few subjects. Detailed discussion of these advanced methods is beyond the scope of this book.

Chapter 6

TOOLS FOR APPLICATIONS

In this chapter I describe several general approaches for aiding human factors evaluations and for developing and presenting design requirements. *Tools* in this context includes concepts for organizing and presenting information and various media for presenting these concepts, including paper; film; electronic presentations and storage systems for published information; computer programs that yield graphics, text, or numbers; and a variety of physical devices, among which are templates, models, and entire mockups of work spaces. Each of these concepts and media will be addressed here, though the presentation in this chapter is brief, broadly applicable to many different application arenas, and rather abstract. Chapters 7, 8, and 9 present application-specific illustrations and discussions showing how such tools are used.

Although there appears to be a bewildering array of options in application techniques, the subject matter may be simply organized in the form of a two-dimensional orthogonal matrix. One dimension is represented by a short list of concepts for analysis and presentation of design requirements; the other dimension is represented by the different types of media. The individual cells of the matrix contain information about which media are appropriate for implementation of the concepts, considering technical feasibility, available funds, schedules, and personnel skills.

As you read this chapter, keep in mind that each of the approaches suggested is part of a system, and that without the complete set of system components, an individual concept and its implementing medium are of little value. For example, describing people in terms of reduced-scale, articulated drafting manikins implies that there are engineering drawings of the same scale on which to overlay the manikins to make human factors evaluations. Similarly, a computer-generated, animated, three-dimensionally defined manikin is of little use without a CAD definition (or other computer-generated image) of a work space within which it can interact and simulate vision, reach, and potential problems of clearance, or be used to develop summary envelopes of reach and clearance requirements. Likewise, envelopes generated in this manner are meaningless apart from the associated definition of work space geometry and a description of the population and particular manikins used to generate the envelopes.

Several of the media have both 2D and 3D options, each with benefits and disadvantages.

Design Criteria Populations

Basic Anthropometry Specifications

To apply anthropometric data, you must first assemble and make selections of the specific data that are most appropriate to the application. It is rare to find exactly the right set of data for any specific new application, especially if the project is complex. In trying to match the potential users of a planned design, you need careful judgment and extensive, detailed comparisons of the individual measurements and demographic characteristics of persons described in published survey reports. However, it may be possible to find a set of measurements that are nearly acceptable, in which case, you may supplement and adjust the data using the estimating and forecasting methods described in Chapter 5 to arrive at a description of a design criteria population — those dimensional criteria you will use for developing design requirements. In some applications, particularly military contract work, published specifications define body dimension limits or percentiles that the contracting agency imposes on the designer. These regulatory documents also must be obtained and used as appropriate in developing design requirements.

The media for basic data and specifications are usually either printed paper (in the form of books, reports, and technical articles) or microfilm. However, some records of anthropometric surveys are available — through the National Technical Information Service (NTIS) or directly from a cognizant government agency — as electronic records in the form of computer tapes or diskettes. In a few cases, regulatory documents, such as MIL-STD-1472, are available from commercial sources as a software package in the hypertext mode. The future may see data and specifications published in many different ways. Today presentations are commonly numerical tabulations, graphs, or charts and may include illustrations of how dimensions were measured.

In Chapters 4 and 5, I discussed the value and use of cumulative normal probability graphs and regressions for data reporting and estimation; these important forms of presentations can be used for applications as well. With modern software they can be presented electronically (on a video display terminal) as well as on paper or plastic film. As requirement definitions, they may be marked with selected limit conditions for design.

Nomographs (also called *nomograms*) are less common forms of graphical presentation that enable you to determine results from several related variables without calculation. Using such presentations usually requires that a straightedge be aligned with two tick marks. Interpolation is often needed to read scales that may not have uniform scale markings. Analog data presentations were popular before the advent of small hand calculators and microcomputers with software for spreadsheets and capabilities for compactly storing copious data in digital form. Ergonomists reading the older literature may encounter nomographs and should be aware of their purposes and value. However, I will not delve into the complex art and science of constructing such presentations; there are books in engineering sections of most libraries that do this very well.

Comprehensive Compilations

One of the most comprehensive collections of anthropometric data published in one set of documents in the English language is contained in two of the three volumes comprising NASA Reference Publication 1024 (Anthropology Research Project staff, 1978a, 1978b, 1978c). Volume I contains a comparative set of data for a wide variety of populations, a predicted set of dimensions for a 1985 astronaut population, and many chapters on different aspects of anthropometry. Volume II presents measured data on 61 military and civilian populations. In all, 295 dimensions are defined and illustrated. Numerical data for each measurement are arranged in tabular format and grouped alphabetically by title. For each dimension, there is a computer order number by which it is identified and a list of surveys in which dimensions were listed. Included are means, standard deviations, coefficients of variation, and selected percentiles for each dimension for those populations on which it was measured. Unfortunately, coefficients of correlation are lacking. Volume III is an extensive bibliography.

Additional data collections appear in a variety of military reports, textbooks, and human factors handbooks, such as those listed in Table 3. From these reference manuals, annotated bibliographies of the government laboratories, and books such as Roebuck et al. (1975) or Pheasant (1986), you can obtain further references to original sources, most of which are reports published by one of the military services. Annotated lists of anthropometric data publications offered by NTIS are also particularly helpful. The Crew Systems Ergonomics Information Analysis Center (CSERIAC), a government agency located at Wright-Patterson Air Force Base, Ohio, is chartered to supply data on human factors or to put people into contact with those who have such data. Additional sources are available in many different languages from other nations. One of the most comprehensive in Europe is that of Ergodata in the Laboratoire Appliquée d'Anthropologie, University René Descartes Paris V, France.

TABLE 3
Selected Anthropometric Data Source Documents

Title and Contents	Reference and Type/ Military or Civilian
A Collation of Anthropometry An extensive comparative compilation of measurements on a large number of anthropometric surveys throughout the world. Strongly emphasizes military populations.	Garrett and Kennedy (1971) Mainly military
A Collation of United States Air Force Anthropometry A limited collection of anthropometric data of USAF personnel.	Kennedy (1986) Military populations
Annotated Bibliography of Applied Physical Anthropology in Human Engineering Abstracts, tabulated data, figures, and charts from 121 references. Total number of references: 149. A collection of relatively unusual sources of early data.	Hansen, Cornog, and Hertzberg (1958) Military and civilian
Anthropometric Source Book. Volume I: Anthropometry for Designers Presents a wide-ranging overview of anthropometry, selected data on several populations, and a forecast of NASA astronauts for the year 1985.	Anthropology Research Project staff (1978a) Military and civilian
Anthropometric Source Book. Volume II: A Handbook of Anthropometric Data One of the most complete data compilations, covering populations from many lands, and presenting a large number of body dimensions as available from the surveys used. Includes means, standard deviations, coefficients of variation, and selected percentiles in compact tabular form, alphabetically by name of measurement.	Anthropology Research Project staff (1978b) Military and civilian
Anthropometrics for Designers A limited collection of data, some of special interest to clothing designers, such as a section on growth rates of different body parts and on somatotyping. Contains some work space layout data and design recommendations.	Croney (1971) Military and civilian
Bodyspace — Anthropometry, Ergonomics and Design Several tables of anthropometric data for British adults and children,	Pheasant (1986) Military and civilian

(continued)

TABLE 3 (continued)

Title and Contents	Reference and Type/ Military or Civilian
and adults from the U.S., France, Germany, Sweden, Switzerland, Poland, Japan, Hong Kong (Chinese), and India. Special populations: Elderly. Also includes many applications data and methods.	
Military Handbook, Anthropometry of U.S. Military Personnel (Metric) (DOD-HDBK-743A) A large collection of anthropometric data for military design applications.	U.S. Department of Defense (1991) Military data
Ethnic Variables in Human Factors Engineering Three chapters focus on anthropometric differences in world populations. (1) Population differences in dimensions; (2) Anthropometric measurements on selected populations of the world; (3) International anthropometric variability and its effect on aircraft cockpit design.	Chapanis (1975) Military and civilian
Humanscale 1/2/3 Contains summaries of anthropometric design data in highly graphic, unusual format: colored plastic sheets and moving data exposed in windows.	Diffrient, Tilley, and Bardagjy (1974) Mix of military and civilian
International Data on Anthropometry Presents a consistent set of tables, each with the same, but small number of dimensions for 21 different groups of populations in the world. Huge bibliography, but basis of estimations for some of the data is not well defined.	Jurgens, Aune, and Pieper (1990) Military and civilian
Man-Systems Integration Standards (NASA-STD-3000) Includes forecasted body dimensions for American male astronauts (based on military data) and Japanese female astronauts (based on civilian clothing study) for year 2000 AD. Handbook format presents only tables of means, 5th and 95th percentiles. Also contains data on mass properties and other concerns of space flight.	NASA (1986) Military and civilian

TABLE 3 (continued)

Title and Contents	Reference and Type/ Military or Civilian
MIL-STD-1472D A collection of data for military populations, combined into tables offered for design limits as 5th to 95th percentiles. Caution should be used when interpreting these data, especially regarding statistical combinations and extrapolations.	U.S. Department of Defense (1989) Military
The Human Body in Equipment Design A very large collection of anthropometric data for engineering design forms the major part of the text. Also contains a variety of other human engineering data and design recommendations.	Damon, Stoudt, and McFarland (1966) Military and civilian data
The Measure of Man A collection of charts and organized, stylized design dimensions for work space layout by industrial designers. Mainly a set of design recommendations.	Dreyfuss (1971) Civilian, based on military surveys
1988 Anthropometric Survey of U.S. Army Personnel: Methods and Summary Statistics Contains the means, standard deviations, coefficients of variation, frequency distributions, measures of skewness and kurtosis, percentiles, and descriptions of how measurements were made on a large sample (1774 men and 2208 women) of the U.S. Army. Data includes 132 standard measurements, 60 derived dimensions, and 48 head and face dimensions collected with an automated headboard. Although constrained to data on a single survey, this is the latest, most complete set of data on Americans in a military service. Data are consistent for males and females and provide an excellent example of how the included types of survey data should be be reported. (Separate documents, listed below, provide data from the same survey relating to coefficients of correlation, regressions, and bivariate distributions).	Gordon et al. (1989b) Military
1988 Anthropometric Survey of U.S. Army Personnel: Pilot Summary Statistics Similar measurements to those listed above for a subset of Army pilots.	Donelson and Gordon (1991) Military

(continued)

TABLE 3 (continued)

Title and Contents	Reference and Type/ Military or Civilian
1988 Anthropometric Survey of U.S. Army Personnel: Correlation Coefficients and Regression Equations	Military personnel
Part 2, Simple and Partial Correlation Tables - Male	Cheverud et al. (1990a)
Part 3, Simple and Partial Correlation Tables - Female	Cheverud et al. (1990b)
Part 4, Bivariate Regression Tables	Cheverud et al. (1990c)
Part 5, Stepwise and Standard Multiple Regression Tables	Cheverud et al. (1990d)
This collection of reports contains data on the 1988 survey of the U.S. Army as noted in the titles.	
Hand Anthropometry of the U.S. Army Personnel Another special report of measurements taken during the 1988 survey. The latest and most extensive hand anthropometry data for a large population.	Greiner (1991) Military
Intercorrelations of Anthropometric Measurements: A Source Book for USA Data One of the few collections of coefficients of correlation for several major surveys of populations in the United States.	Churchill, Kitka, and Churchill (1977) Military and civilian

Special Populations

Besides the adult working populations, military personnel, and college students for which many products are designed, there are many special groups that require as much or more attention and often present unique challenges in the development of anthropometric design requirements. Anthropometric data sources are less comprehensive and rarer for such groups as disabled airline passengers, especially those needing wheelchairs (Architectural and Transportation Barriers Compliance Board, 1982), elderly persons (Annis, Case, Clauser, and Bradtmiller, 1991; Kelly and Kroemer, 1990; Pheasant, 1986), pregnant drivers (Culver and Viano, 1990), children (Snyder, Spencer, Owings, and Schneider, 1975), handicapped farmers (Breaking New Ground Resource Center, 1986), and police. Populations that have been the object of fairly extensive surveys include air traffic controllers (Snow and Snyder, 1965), female airline attendants (Snow, Reynolds, and Allgood, 1975) and bus and truck drivers (Sanders and Shaw, 1985).

Dimensioned Illustrations — Engineering Drawings of People

The foregoing data compilations are essential application tools for human factors personnel, but you still have to develop presentations that describe the shape and capability of individuals and populations of people in ways that are readily understood by designers. Many engineers and industrial designers think in pictures more easily and comfortably than they deal with purely numerical or verbally expressed abstract concepts, especially for applications dealing with 3D relationships of human-machine interfaces.

Among the most basic types of tools recommended here are 2D illustrations of a passive nature, typically pencilled or inked on paper or on a thin plastic translucent or transparent film. These are traditionally called *engineering drawings*. Equally useful in today's computer-literate society are screen displays in CAD software formats. Printouts or plots of electronic presentations are often in the form of engineering drawings. The following discussion of graphics is generally applicable, to the extent that such CAD techniques simply make the 2D, static media quicker or easier to create, modify, and replicate or to enhance with color, shading, or other special effects. Dynamic and animated illustrations of 3D objects, such as figures spinning around on a computer screen, will be discussed later.

Orthographic engineering drawings were originally developed for machinery and construction projects. However, the techniques can and should be used for describing human figures (also for defining human space requirements, envelopes of reach and clearance, and other anthropometric evaluations to be described later). Engineers often begin with scale drawings called layouts, which serve to check calculated dimensions, prove the adequacy of data to define the shapes, and possibly even help to define some contours and dimensions through the practiced eye and logical analysis of the drafter. These are then converted into detail and assembly drawings that present dimensions in the form of numbers associated with arrows showing distances on three-view outline drawings. An example is shown in Figure 29. This medium can be an important aid in the development of requirements and to provide design guidance. A valuable benefit inherent in the process of preparing engineering drawings is the discipline required to assemble data systematically and organize them into complete, visual body forms. Ideally, if you are planning an anthropometric survey, you should perform this drawing exercise using hypothetical numbers as a method for systematically identifying which dimensions are essential to create design criteria. My experiences with this activity have led to another benefit: learning and organizing the estimation methods in Chapter 5.

An important message that engineering drawings should convey is that designers should accommodate people whose dimensions fall between the maximum and minimum lengths listed for each dimension. A more subtle,

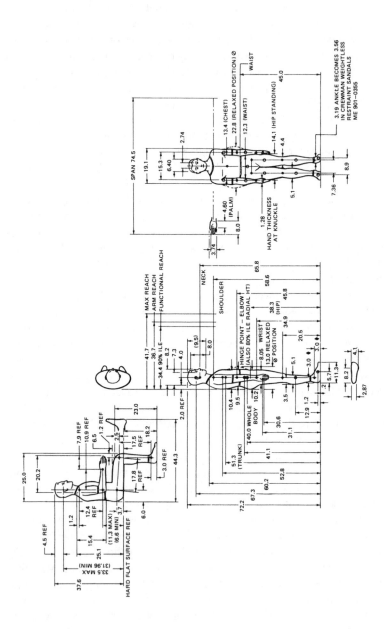

Figure 29. Example of basic body dimension drawing for work space design (courtesy of Space Division, Rockwell International Corporation).

but also important, message is that the persons preparing these drawings need to understand the way engineers think and be able to speak their language. Thus, engineering drawings may influence engineers to accept the human factors recommendations that accompany them.

Of great intuitive value in such presentations is their ability to show dimensions without using technical terms of anatomy and anthropology that are usually unfamiliar to persons in other disciplines, especially engineers and designers. However, in preparing drawings, you must not fall into the trap of promoting the concepts of "the average man" or "the 95th percentile woman," neither of which exists (Annis and McConville, 1990). One approach is to dimension drawings as if they represent parts to be manufactured, with a tolerance on each dimension, rather than a single number. Tolerances are determined by the selected range of percentiles used as design criteria. The rules for applying these tolerances should be carefully defined to users in a way that explains the potential for individual variability of each dimension. Most body dimensions are correlated, so additional information must be provided about realistic trend information (such as regression relationships), so that designs based on these types of drawings do not result in some adjustments and sizes of equipment that are extremely unlikely and thus uneconomical.

Another approach is to compile drawings of a set of worst-case combinations of dimensions, such as the six required for some Navy contracts or the eight recommended by some Air Force contracts. Further discussion of this boundary condition approach appears later in relation to the design of drafting manikins and the use of principal component analysis for developing computer-generated human models.

The drawings prepared by Henry Dreyfuss (1971) and his associates (Diffrient, Tilley, and Bardagjy, 1974; Diffrient, Tilley, and Harman, 1981) are excellent examples of almost fully graphical presentations. In concept, these drawings are relatively easy to understand and essential for users such as designers, whose livelihood and way of thinking depend on the visual expression of ideas. However, the statistical bases for the data presented in these references — particularly Humanscale 1/2/3 — have not been fully and properly documented. Be sure to check the data against original reports before applying them to designs.

This discussion provides another insight:

> **A complete set of anthropometic methods must encompass concepts of user-friendly, industry-appropriate presentations of data and criteria for design, as well as measuring and manipulating statistics on body dimensions.**

Substitute Human Forms

Among the very useful engineering aids to work space, clothing, and personal equipment design are accurately scaled, physical models of human beings. These range from simple, 2D forms for design layout and analysis on drafting paper to 3D, instrumented anthropomorphic dummies for testing escape systems and restraint harnesses. They provide powerful working tools for assembling the aforementioned data in ways that aid visualization of general spatial relationships and at the same time act as precision tools for measuring and evaluating numerical data of concern to human factors analysis and design. Following are some examples.

Drafting Manikins (2D)

Articulated, transparent sheet plastic manikins are useful when the design media are paper and pencil. A set of manikins is commonly prepared in a range of sizes and scales (ranging from 1/20th to full size) for use in a design department. These devices are usually made to represent 2D aspects of a man or woman as seen from the side, such as shown in Figure 30. However, some may also represent a fore-aft view, plan view, or other aspect.

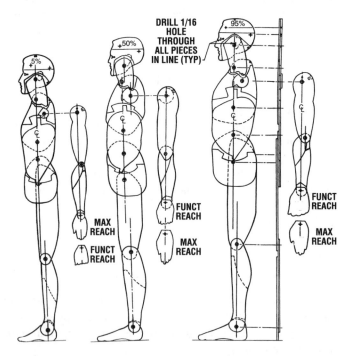

Figure 30. Articulated drafting manikins (after Carlyle, 1960;
courtesy of McDonnell Douglas Corporation).

Because of the limited quantities usually required, the cost for each manikin generally has been high. The analysis and preparation of engineering drawings of such devices can involve extensive and costly engineering time. Furthermore, they are frequently made by skilled model makers, largely by hand. If possible, use an existing design or obtain a commercially available product. Currently, a small number of different types can be obtained ready-made from vendors (Berol Corporation, 1976; Kennedy, 1989; Rogers, 1976).

For large and complex design projects, even a newly developed set of drafting manikins may have benefits that far outweigh the costs because they allow the study of many positioning options with minimal drawing time. Another benefit is that drafters who are not well trained in drawing the human figure can produce professional results by tracing around such devices. Finally, drafting manikins are portable and require no electronics or software to operate.

When considering the acquisition or design and fabrication of a set of articulated manikins, the following factors should be taken into account: (1) the number, type, and size of the manikins required to do the job; (2) the degree of fidelity required; and (3) the acceptability of available designs versus the cost of developing new ones. For maximum flexibility, a large number of sizes and scales is desirable. For example, you might want manikins representing a selected set of worst-case combinations of body dimensions. One set may depict minimally clothed operators; another may depict operators in bulky cold-weather gear or space suits. Separate manikins might be needed to represent male and female operators. Scales selected might include 1/20, 1/10, 1/4, and 1/2 scale. Although I have emphasized that no single person in a population can have all dimensions with the same percentile rank, manikins used in the past have been prepared from a selected set of key dimensions having the same percentile. If properly used as gauges of *one dimension at a time*, manikins are still a convenient way to represent design criteria, such as the 5th, 50th, and 95th percentiles of the key dimensions.

If you are planning to design and develop drafting manikins with new custom shapes and sizes, be sure to review the 15-step procedure presented by Roebuck et al. (1975, pp. 219–220). The procedure begins with the establishment of the population dimension statistics and carries through to final inspection of the fabricated parts. It includes integrating a wide range of published data (and other data as available) and exercising many of the anthropometric methods described elsewhere in this book. Even with guidance like this, designers must be knowledgeable about the methods discussed in Chapter 5 and experienced in anthropometry and anatomy in order to use drafting manikins successfully.

Electronic, 2D manikins can be (and have been) developed for CAD applications, based on the same analytical processes used in the development of physical manikins. Electronic manikins are manipulated using a mouse, trackball, or equivalent device and keyboard on a computer, assuming the software has been developed and is available.

Dummies and Manikins (3D)

Anthropometric dummies (examples of which appear in Chapters 7 and 9) of various types may be constructed as the 3D counterparts of drafting manikins, either as physical devices or as computer models. Physical, full-scale human forms can be used for visualization and to check dimensional clearance during design development in 3D mockups. Likewise, small-scale models are useful for visualizing space relationships in models of work and occupancy sites. Such cases may result in significant cost avoidance.

Full-scale dummies are usually required for dynamic or static force simulations. These simulations may include studies of bed comfort, seating posture, and comfort (Kohara and Sugi, 1972; Roe, 1993), crash safety, ejection demonstrations, and work space verifications. Dynamic test dummies for crash demonstrations must be constructed of high-strength materials such as steel, ceramics, and tough plastics. They must also provide interior cavities for measurement and recording instruments, possibly telemetering devices, and batteries or other power sources. Their joints are typically designed with devices to simulate joint movement resistance and/or muscle forces. Simulation of joint range of motion limits and stiffness frequently is a key concern. Other anthropometric problems are shape factors affecting wind drag, mass properties of body segments, and clearances during ejections or movements during simulated crashes.

For thermal studies, the physical characteristics of dummy materials require different characteristics to simulate human skin and perhaps perspiration and heat capacity. Anthropometric design criteria for such dummies should focus on accuracy of total body area, radiation area, and mass properties.

Different forms of dummies are often used to simulate effects of ionizing radiation on internal organs. For these applications, the density and chemical properties of materials, shape factors of internal volumes, and external dimensions are significant. Such dummies are often called *phantoms* and are generally cast in a specific posture. Phantoms have no moving parts.

Three-dimensional dummies, also called manikins, and parts of these forms — such as heads, hands, and feet — are used to assist in the design and fit-testing of torso clothing and headgear. (More about these applications appears in Chapter 9.) If the purpose is merely to demonstrate range of motion, low-density materials may be employed in models such as described by Dempster (1955). Models of this type may have little or no flesh representation but consist mainly of tubes and joint mechanisms.

Multimedia Measurement and Replication Methods

Dummies and other 3D physical representations can be produced in several ways. Traditionally the process includes measurement, data analysis, and design, followed by fabrication in a shop. Alternative processes can combine measurement directly with design and fabrication through a variety of electronic and machining or chemical media. These systems include one or more sensor units and a process for converting sensed information into digital data. The data are then used to fabricate sculptures. Some processes use mechanical cutters, sometimes driven by computer programs. Others produce 3D solid objects by light polymerization of a chemical, a process called *stereolithography*. This process uses laser beams under the control of a computer to solidify a plastic gel mixture, layer by layer. As the object is slowly submerged in a vat of the plastic gel, each layer is bonded to the layer below to form complex scale models.

Another computer-controlled buildup process that is also available uses dry powder for the initial material (Gregor, 1994). A machine deposits successive layers of the powder on a surface. Then an ink-jet printhead deposits a binder that solidifies the powder into a ceramic within the designated cross-section shape for each layer. The process is repeated until all necessary layers of a mold are formed. Then the layers are assembled and fired, and molten metal is poured into the mold to form the finished product.

Although these desktop manufacturing methods are very expensive, costs may decrease as the technology is improved and demand for the products increases.

Computer-Generated Human Models

Computer models of humans are among the most recent technology innovations for evaluations of human-machine-environment interactions. As considered here, they are generally more complex than drafting manikins, more like electronic counterparts of the physical manikins described above, generally represented in three dimensions, and have many attributes defined for them, such as mass properties, three-axis ranges of motion of joints, view points (representing eyes), color, and strength. The good news about this technique is that these models permit early evaluations of preliminary designs in three dimensions prior to the construction of mockups and in a variety of later evaluations of such activities as maintenance (Boyle et al., 1991; Gross, 1991; Majoros, 1990; Roebuck, 1991; Scott, 1991). Other long-range benefits or by-products are that they present extremely challenging and interesting new problems for research and design in this technology. The discipline of devising computer-generated models in a systematic manner creates new approaches to solving these problems, and the resulting solutions will likely lead to new systematizations of knowledge and quantification of information that may benefit all anthropometric applications.

The bad news about this technique is that humans are highly complex, widely variable creatures and very difficult to model, even using complex mathematical approaches. For the near term, anthropometrists and other human factors specialists must struggle with great shortages of appropriate digital data on even the limited features of human size, shape, and capability that should be modeled. Before using a computer-generated model, you should investigate the data and assumptions on which it is based and understand how they are used so that you can assess the benefits and limitations of the model. Pay particular attention to the statistical derivations in the anthropometry and to the algorithms that control movement of limbs and trunk. In some cases, documentation is inadequate, data are used incorrectly, or models have not been validated, so that the results from applying the model are questionable.

What does a computer model do? In a metaphorical sense, it reconstitutes and animates human body forms from a set of anthropometric and biomechanical data. Physical anthropologists and engineering anthropometrists have for decades attempted to describe the essences of body form and motion capability with a few numbers gained from point-to-point measurements. But computer science now provides a method of breathing a type of simulated life and substance into such numbers in the form of animated screen representations of human forms at work and play in two and three dimensions. These forms can be made to interact with electronically represented environments, tools, equipment, and clothing. Thus, computer models can, in a sense, reconstitute these mathematically defined persons and employ them in useful ways to simulate what real people might be able to do and thereby identify difficulties people may have in carrying out certain tasks.

A great many partial and whole-body computer models have been devised for various applications. Some of the most promising recent approaches were summarized in the proceedings of a workshop on the subject in 1986 (Kroemer, Snook, Meadows, and Deutsch, 1988). However, in the last several years, there has been a quantum leap in the diversity and amount of activity in this field. Significant advances have been made in such diverse fields as multivariate analysis for setting design requirements and for design evaluation, new approaches for geometric descriptions, improved user interfaces, mathematical methods for defining strength and motion, computer languages, highly versatile computer graphics, and software for interactions with computer-aided design. The following discussion is limited to advances in multivariate statistics and interactions between validations and applications procedures.

Many of the early computer models were aimed at producing manikins representing commonly specified percentiles, such as the 5th, 50th, or 95th percentile, as was commonly done for drafting manikins. That is, each model came in sizes, with as many possible dimensions at the same percentile rating. Many currently used and promoted models are still based on this approach. Of course, their validity for design is just as limited and questionable as for the drafting manikins. Several authors have calculated how many people would really be accommodated by such models in tight work spaces. The results are disturbing: The percentage of persons accommodated falls off rapidly as more critical dimensions are considered (Annis and McConville, 1990; Bittner, Dannhaus, and Roth, 1975; Roebuck et al., 1975). Consequently, modeling approaches have been developed that permit the power of computers to be applied in a way that more realistically represents the wide diversity of possible percentiles that can occur in a population. These approaches currently represent the cutting edge of anthropometric application technology, and serious students of the subject should become familiar with them.

It is beyond the scope of this book to describe in depth the mathematical bases for these generation processes. The results, however, permit users to move from the evaluation of what specific percentiles are accommodated to evaluation of what percentage of persons in a sample (and thus, by implication, the percentage of an entire population) will be accommodated. This is really what the use of percentiles was intended to accomplish in design practice.

Principal Component Analysis

One approach that aims at adapting the specific sizes in a more sophisticated manner involves calculating certain statistically feasible worst-case examples (Meindl et al., 1993; Zehner et al., 1993). This method depends on principal component analysis (PCA) to develop a set of boundary conditions (limits for a selected few measurements) for a multidimensional distribution of human measurements. These boundary conditions are much better able to guarantee a given percentage of accommodation in a design than are common-percentile manikins.

This powerful tool could be used to define dimensions of a set of drafting manikins or even a dimensioned illustration, rather than a comprehensive computer graphics model. As a practical matter, however, computer analysis is needed to use PCA in a timely manner. As a tool, PCA is like a fixed-size gauge used for inspection in machinery manufacturing. It can tell you if the design meets or exceeds the stated criteria, but not by how much it missed if the criteria are not met. A version of this approach is currently used by the Safework human modeling program (Genicom Consultants, 1993).

Monte Carlo Generation

Another approach, of a more general nature, was described by Bittner (1975) in a model called *computerized accommodated percentage evaluation* (CAPE) and later incorporated into the Crewstation Assessment of Reach (CAR) model (Harris, Bennett, and Dow, 1980) and the McDonnell Douglas Human Modeling System (MDHMS). In these models the user can ask the program to generate, by Monte Carlo methods, a set of synthetic operator stick models that have different percentiles for each dimension. The selection of percentiles is governed by software that generates random multipliers of the standard deviations that are constrained by correlation coefficients between all pairs of dimensions and by the means and standard deviations of each dimension's distribution. It is assumed that all dimensions are normally distributed. The result of this procedure is to produce dimensions for a large set of synthetic operators (typically 400 to 3600), each having dimensions of varying percentiles within the manikin design and each dimension statistically distributed with essentially the same means and standard deviations and with all pairs of dimensions correlated approximately to the same degree as the original population. So, although no single synthetic operator is guaranteed to match a living subject, each operator represents one possible case that could occur in a population of living people without violating any of the underlying statistics. Each operator manikin is then used in a simulation of human activity within a work space geometry. As a tool, this approach is more helpful than that of PCA because it gives a figure of merit that indicates how good the design is, as well as whether or not it meets a particular criterion of percentage accommodation.

Validation Concerns and Application Procedures

An important consideration in using the computer model approach is how carefully the fidelity of the computer model has been validated in representing size, mobility, strength, vision, and other key factors. Although glowing claims have been made for the value of many of the existing computer human models, the fact is that much work is required to improve and extend validation procedures. As a consequence, some agencies (particularly the U.S. Navy) prefer that mockup evaluations be performed with live human subjects. There is still a need for more research and development in this theoretically promising technique so that higher degrees of fidelity can be demonstrated.

A prudent approach to ergonomic evaluation begins with computer modeling to establish the most obvious requirements as early as possible and follows with evaluations of mockups using human subjects. The computer models can be used initially to point out probable areas of controversial fit and functional capability of humans working in the design space. Then a small number of carefully selected and measured human subjects can economically evaluate a few critical mockup conditions to verify the applicability of the model or provide data for upgrading it. Evaluation with live subjects increases confidence that the vehicle or work site is appropriate for use by the intended user population.

Using the data gathered from the mockup study, the computer model can then be upgraded or modified to simulate more precisely the exact limits for design criteria for specified body dimensions and mobility.

Although live subjects seldom can exactly represent anthropometric design goals for all body dimensions of interest, the data gathered from a mockup study can be used to help upgrade a computer model to simulate more accurately the exact limits for specified design criteria, body dimensions, and mobility. Also, each repetition of the cycles for succeeding products should lead to improvements in the computer model and greater confidence that it will provide better electronic evaluations earlier in the design process. Eventually it may be possible to omit most of the early mockup studies using human subjects, saving a great deal of money and time. However, computer simulations using human models still need much development, critical examination, and standardization.

Mockups and Models of Work/Occupancy Spaces

Places where people work or perform other daily functions are often represented by full-scale 3D constructions called *mockups* (other names are used in different industries). Although mockups were invented long before human factors or ergonomics became recognized disciplines, they are now almost indispensable tools for human factors evaluation in many situations. Long experience in several vehicle industries (aircraft, spacecraft, automotive) has proven the value of mockups at different levels of detail and fidelity. I do not have the space to recount the many times in my 40-year career that I have seen how mockups can teach some new truth or provide essential, early, and relatively low-cost verification of design concepts. I strongly advocate the use of computer models to reduce significantly the number and types of preliminary mockups, but I still recommend that critical work space be evaluated with some form of mockup before settling on final designs. The less the planned space resembles common, earthbound, daily situations, the greater is the need for a mockup.

Preliminary, minimal-cost mockups may be cheaply constructed with paper-faced foam plastic, corrugated cardboard, poster board, and even strings or sheet celluloid. Masking tape and duct tape are versatile methods for fastening sheet materials together. These materials can be formed into strong shapes, even providing for seating.

As design development proceeds, mockups may be constructed of plywood, heavy sheet plastics, and sheet metal parts or even pipes, clamps, and machined parts to improve durability and fidelity. In addition to assisting in visualization of a design for engineering feasibility considerations, these more elaborate mockups can also serve diverse needs, including safety considerations, crew performance verifications, maintainability, manufacturing feasibility, marketing, and even early crew training.

Every engineering design and evaluation discipline has different goals for the use of mockups. Systems engineering personnel are interested in the routing of ducts, pipe, cable, and electric wires. Structures personnel are concerned with assembly and strength. The anthropometrist is concerned with where to place reference planes or locator landmarks that can be used for later measurements with live subjects in the experimental space. Some parts of enclosures should be removable so that photographic or video recording or optical sightings for measurements may be easily made. Sometimes a special jig or fixture must be designed to interface with existing mockup surfaces in order to provide for measurements. Examples are shown later in the discussion of aerospacecraft work space design (pages 113–115).

Safety is an important concern in designing and planning the use of mockups with human subjects. Although the materials may be fake, the humans are not. Often it is necessary to support mockups with strong wood platforms, metal plates, tubes, and bars to resist handling loads or to support the weight of subjects.

Because the anthropometrist is often the person most directly involved with mockups in a day-to-day working relationship, he or she may become the de facto spokesperson for a generalized systems engineering point of view regarding many aspects of design.

Frequently, attempts to locate seats or instrument panels correctly will reveal design features that are incompatible with other engineering requirements. The anthropometrist has an obligation to notify the engineering staff about such problems when they are identified.

Except for considerations of safety and strength, much of the foregoing discussion also applies to the use of smaller-scale physical models of work and occupancy sites. Reduced costs and transportability of the model are the most compelling reasons for small-scale models.

The computer age has made possible electronically defined representations of work space geometry that may have many of the 3D visualization benefits formerly available only in physical devices. These representations constitute counterparts of mockups and models that are useful for the early evaluation of concurrent engineering analysis. To be sure, you cannot physically enter these work spaces and feel comfort or discomfort, experience reach difficulties, or evaluate sounds. However, you *can* evaluate them in several ways by placing into them the computer-generated human models described earlier or by visually experiencing some of their aspects with virtual reality systems. These electronic work space representations should be some type of simplified abstraction, rather than the final engineering geometry with all its details. In general, such graphics should be surfaced — that is, hidden lines should be removed and external planes should be rendered as colored surfaces to make them more easily understood.

Envelopes

In addition to descriptions of people and workplaces, it is useful to compile design requirements and prepare analytical tools in 2D and 3D presentations that define the form of spaces that people occupy (clearance envelopes), volumes defining reach limits (reach envelopes), and various other requirements such as needed adjustments in equipment. The media may be engineering drawings, CAD computer screen displays, or other graphics or physical models and mockups. These presentations can help analysts and designers to visualize spaces needed for functional work or other occupancy requirements. They may be thought of as summaries of spatial movement evaluations or swept volumes that relate interactions between people and machinery or buildings.

Reach Envelopes
A commonly needed envelope shows reach limits for the smaller members of a population. It is generally defined as the composite set of surfaces traced by the fingertips of people with short reach measurements (usually 5th percentile) in a functional work posture. For sitting postures, some of the minimum downward reach conditions are defined by persons with short arms and long trunks, one of the likely conditions of differing percentile rankings among real people. Although no single manikin can generate the totality of such reach envelopes, you can successively use short arms on manikins with short trunks and long trunks to generate some of the limiting reach conditions. Other limits, such as access into equipment, may be limited by short arms and deep chest dimensions.

Because reach measurements are highly sensitive to the motivation of subjects and the instructions given to them, caution must be exercised in interpreting and applying reported reach data. The reach described may be "maximally stretched" or "convenient" reach, or determined by some other criteria such as minimum energy, minimum time, accuracy of reach, or limitations of body restraints such as a shoulder harness or bulky clothing.

Reach envelopes may be defined in the form of 2D engineering drawings or computer model simulations in three dimensions. Occasionally a free-standing, physical model will be constructed to illustrate the concept (Human Factors Section, Eastman Kodak Company, 1983). However, rarely would you construct 3D reach envelopes using physical materials and place them in mockups for evaluations. The design and fabrication of these devices, though technically feasible, would have to be complex (and costly) so that they could be folded into a small package for insertion, then expanded toward all surrounding panels and other structural surfaces in a way that would define reachable areas meaningfully.

Clearance Envelopes

Clearance envelopes define volumes within which a designer should not place controls, parts of structures, plumbing, wiring, or other hardware. Larger people generally set these criteria. However, the legs of people with short trunk dimensions may constrain the location of things like control wheels in a cockpit because of the need to maintain all pilots at a given eye height so they can see outside the craft.

As with reach envelopes, clearance requirements for body parts and movements may be shown in a variety of ways for engineering or industrial design applications, including computer-generated graphics. However, clearance envelopes are particularly amenable to depiction as physical representations because they generally do not closely interface with surfaces such as control panels. As shown by examples in Chapter 7, they may be placed in mockups for evaluations. They may depict space required exclusively for people, for motion of things, or for combinations of people handling things, as in maintenance work.

Adjustment and Eye Position Envelopes

Another type of useful model defines the range of adjustment of a designated point on items such as seats or desks, or the range of locations of a key body feature, such as the eyes. In the case of seats in the aircraft industry, the model is oriented relative to a Seat Reference Point (SRP). There are several possible definitions of the SRP, depending on use. One of the best for modeling is the point located on the medial vertical plane at the intersection of the supporting surfaces for the seat back and the seat bottom. For convenience, supporting surfaces are generally defined as theoretical planes tangent to the points of greatest compression of the cushions. Actual cushion compression is slightly different for people of various weights, shapes, densities, and postural preferences and is affected by variations in cushion compression rates. However, an average location is usually determined based on actual measurements or estimated average cushion compressions (often about half the cushion thickness).

For convenience in rigging seat locations during assembly and inspection, SRPs may be defined in terms of a specific rivet or attach bolt or the uncompressed cushion intersections. Designers and ergonomists should be extremely careful in determining which SRP is being referenced in each analysis.

In automotive engineering, an adjustment model would be oriented around what is called the *H-point*, located approximately at the assumed average center between the hip joints of a driver or passenger. Adjustment envelopes that simply define a range for a Seat Reference Point or H-point are generally only lines on paper or electronic outlines in 2D and 3D CAD form. An example is shown in Chapter 7 (page 118).

Because they would occupy the same space as a seat structure, physical, 3D representations of such adjustment envelopes are not practical for mockup evaluations. However, you could define a physical representation of seat adjustment range in terms of a clearance envelope for the outer surfaces of a seat. Such an envelope could be very useful in demonstrating potential interferences with other items in a work space.

Chapter 7 includes further discussion of eye position envelopes in relation to automotive interior design.

Chapter 7

WORK SPACE DESIGN AND EVALUATION

Work space, for the purposes of this chapter, means all types of compartments, cockpits, rooms, offices, automobiles, boats, spacecraft, factory assembly stations, and maintenance activity sites. Work space may involve machinists in stationary situations or individuals in nonworking postures, even including airline passengers sleeping in a reclined seat. Although I admit that this definition of work space may be a bit misleading, it obviates the need for awkward and vague modifiers such as *occupancy* or *environmental* or the need for a great many specific modifiers — such as *resting*, *eating*, *voiding*, *grooming*, and *working* — that collectively may still not be comprehensive.

I will cite specific applications for only a few types of vehicles and stationary workstations, but you should think of them as instances of general principles, applicable to many designed and fabricated objects and spaces encountered in daily life. A recommended sequence of steps is illustrated by the flowchart in Figure 31 (Roebuck et al., 1975), using terminology common to the aerospace industry. Different industries and areas of application may use other terminology and elect to apply only some of the procedures. Note that the activities involving anthropometric methods are represented by rectangles with solid outlines. Some of these activities will be referenced in the examples that follow.

To set the theme of the following discussion, I use the analogy of *installation engineering* from industrial practice. The fundamental problem faced by any equipment installation engineer is to ensure that adequate volume, clearance, attachments, supports, and system connections are provided so that the equipment may operate as intended. Designing and evaluating work spaces for humans should receive equally thorough analysis. Unfortunately, often it does not, partly because the engineers in charge of accommodations have little training in human factors and do not understand the need to provide adequately for humans.

Here I provide some of that often missing knowledge, particularly as it relates to the geometric aspects of design requirements that account for human variability. Evaluation is an integral part of the process, both for refining requirements and for determining whether the ergonomic goals of the design are being met. However, there are many anthropometric evalua-

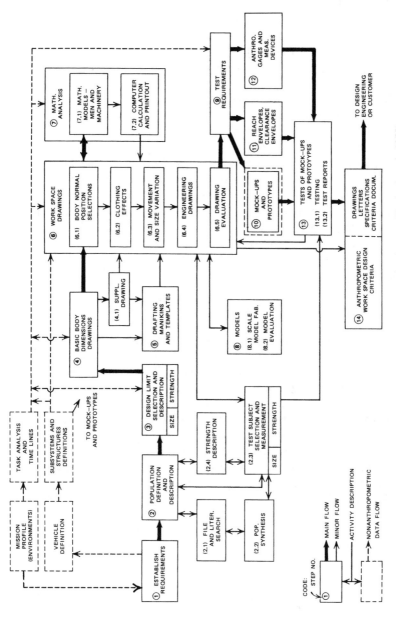

Figure 31. Flowchart of procedures in work space development (Roebuck et al., 1975).

103

tions that appear very similar in methodology but for which the goal is simply the selection or screening of operators for machines that have already been put in production, possibly many years previously.

A Work Space Paradigm: The Aerospacecraft Control Station

The first example is the design of a control station in a space vehicle in which the crew experiences an unusual set of conditions, ranging from microgravity (weightlessness) to the high loads of launch from the earth (rather than, say, from the moon), atmospheric entry, and splashdown. The costs of weight for internal components (seats, for instance) and the structure for interior pressurization are very high. In addition, weightlessness creates special problems. These factors require a fresh, critical look at every aspect of design accommodations, far beyond what is practical or economical for more conventional human activities. The insights so gained may even help to improve the design of simpler and more familiar work sites. Let us follow the steps in Figure 31 to show how they are applied to the development of a spacecraft crew station.

Step 1. Establish Requirements

Before beginning an actual work space layout, you need to determine mission and system design requirements (Roebuck et al., 1975):

1. Purpose or mission of the system. Example: "Land men on the moon before 1970 and return them safely to earth."
2. Mission profile, a detailed description of phases and environments in a typical or critical mission. Example: "Launch vertically, accelerate to 4.5 G, orbit earth (weightless), accelerate to 1 G to transonic coast flight (weightless)," and so forth through the entire mission.
3. Tolerances allowable in the performance of the system (limits of accuracy, speed, force, etc.). Examples: Launch time, aiming accuracy, re-entry velocity, accelerative force limits, oxygen consumption rates, atmospheric pressures.
4. Effects on system performance if tolerances are not met.
5. Vehicle concept definition: Geometry and dimensions, location of functional work areas, fundamental structural characteristics.

Environment and Orientation Effects

One of the major system requirements for any work space design is a definition of the general environment and orientation of the occupant or operator.

Severe thermal or toxic environments call for protective clothing (e.g., a space suit) that adds to the bulk of nude body dimensions and limits effective ranges of joint motion. Accelerative forces may require a seated posture and restraint belts or even a supine posture (used in current spacecraft) for the launch mode.

Figure 32 illustrates a lesson learned from the design of a spacecraft couch: Distances from the back of the thighs or seat pan to the top of the head and shoulders become longer in the supine posture. When the body reclines, reduced gravitational forces along the spine change the length of the spinal column and allow some flesh expansion. Both a good night's rest on earth and weightlessness in space travel produce some spinal elongation, but the long-term changes of microgravity generally produce much more (Anthropology Research Project staff, 1978a). In general, postural changes require allowances for body dimensions that differ from those measured in standard anthropometric postures. In most cases, the modifications are additions to external diameters or lengths, but they may sometimes be reductions, such as in "slumped" postures for sitting.

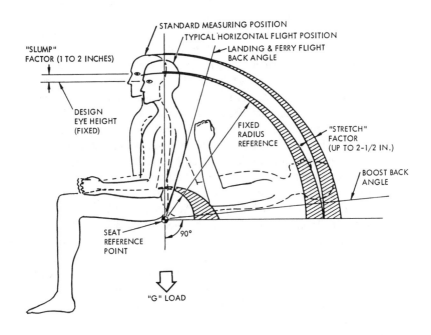

Figure 32. Trunk length and eye-to-seat dimensions change with body attitude (Roebuck et al., 1975).

Major challenges in spacecraft design derive from the extremes of accelerative forces and thermal environments, for which various forms of special protection are needed. To meet pressure and thermal protection requirements, space suits create new interfaces between human and machine. Extremes of the work environment and skill needs have led to specific selection criteria, creating a need for a definition of new populations called *astronauts* in the United States and *cosmonauts* in the former USSR. These new populations have body dimensions that differ from the larger national populations from which they come.

Step 2. Population Definition and Description

As I explained in Chapter 6, definition of the operator population is a key concern at the start of a project involving humans. For the *Apollo* project, crew skill and selection requirements were met by military test pilots with extensive test flight experience and in excellent physical condition. The most appropriate anthropometric survey appeared to be that of U.S. Air Force flying personnel referred to earlier in this book (Hertzberg et al., 1954). The wide variations in these measurements suggested a design specification that each couch should be adjustable to accommodate whatever person was assigned to a flight, much as in a military or commercial aircraft.

This policy was different from that for the earlier *Mercury* project, in which each couch was custom-formed for only one pilot. Nevertheless, it was still necessary to consider sizing for each of the astronauts selected by NASA up to the time that design of the *Apollo* command module was started, because all were almost certainly going to be on at least one of the flights. Fortunately, each astronaut had been measured in considerable detail as part of his selection process, and the data were made available to the spacecraft design teams. The *Mercury* astronauts were graduates of test pilot school, had active service as military pilots with at least 1500 hours of flying time, and were in excellent physical condition. Only males between 25 and 40 years of age with a bachelor's degree and under 180 cm in height (5 ft. 11 in.) were accepted (Swenson, Grimwood, and Alexander, 1966).

After Project *Apollo*, when it became apparent that spacecraft design and fabrication was likely to be a decade-long development process, I saw that forecasting of anthropometric criteria was necessary to define the population of operators. My recommendation to perform forecasting was accepted by NASA for the development of design criteria for the space shuttle. Forecasting has also been used in planning for the Space Station *Freedom* design studies (Roebuck et al., 1988).

Another concern related to the process of population definition and description is the search for and selection of subjects from within the staff of the design organization. Naturally, these persons must be selected to match certain cases of combinations of body dimensions that represent criteria for design, such as selected upper and lower percentiles or other combinations of perhaps midrange percentiles that would constrain clearance, vision, or reach. They also need to be thoroughly measured during selection or as they are used in mockup demonstrations and evaluation.

Step 3. Design Limits Selection and Numerical Description

After the characteristics of the user population are defined, the next step is to define how many people and what range of percentiles will be used as design criteria. This decision establishes the theoretical design limits for those to be accommodated and constitutes what is called a *design criteria population*. Mathematically precise ways of integrating economic and political considerations into this decision have yet to be devised. However, the usual practice is to select some large range of accommodation, such as 5th–95th percentiles. For Project *Apollo*, the criteria were set at 10th–90th percentiles for certain key dimensions and 5th–95th for others. The key dimensions were "standing height, weight, sitting height-erect, buttock-knee length, knee height-sitting, hip breadth-sitting, shoulder breadth-bideltoid, and arm reach from wall" (Roebuck et al., 1975). In order for each man to fit any couch in the command module, each of the three couches was made to adjust for all men meeting these criteria. Today you might use Monte Carlo methods for analysis, the results of which might lead you to open up the design criteria to a wider range of percentiles.

The *Apollo* criteria were generous by Project *Mercury* standards, but not so in light of later data. The first flight of *Apollo* was on October 11, 1968, 18 years after the 1950 survey of Air Force flying personnel. In the meantime, the 90th-percentile Stature had risen from 183.38 cm to 185.17 cm in 1967. It is not surprising that there were strong recommendations to raise the upper selection limit for crews to 185 cm.

Step 4. Preparation of Engineering Drawings of Basic Body Dimensions

Though not essential, this step (or its technical equivalent in other documentation) is strongly recommended. A three-view drawing that shows minimum and maximum dimension limits of the population with the body in standard anthropometric postures is desirable for reviewing the completeness of dimensions, for ease of reference in planning changes, and for conducting quick checks of design layouts. For work space design, particular emphasis should be placed on lengths, breadths, and depths rather than on circumferences. An example of portions of such a drawing was shown in Figure 29 (page 88). This step begins a process of systematic compilation and documentation of data that lead to specific design requirements and provide a basis for the design of manikins or for programming computer models, if these are to be used.

Step 5. Preparation of Drafting Aids

During Project *Apollo*, a set of articulated drafting manikins, like those described in Chapter 6, was designed and fabricated for spacecraft interior designers to use in analyzing engineering drawings. These included depictions of body forms in shirt sleeves and in pressure suits. With current computer technology, these simulations of the human form could be simple, 2D CAD depictions for quick analysis of preliminary designs. However, it is better to use solid geometry computer graphics and to use 3D computer human models for early design. For the design of Space Station *Freedom*, several computer human models are being used. Among them are Jack® (Badler, Phillips, and Webber, 1993; developed at the University of Pennsylvania) and MDHMS, the McDonnell Douglas Human Modeling System (see Scott, 1991, on DHMS, the former name).

Step 6. Preparation of Work Space Layouts

This is the step in which design criteria are actually applied to design geometry. A nondimensioned but accurately scaled layout is prepared for the major geometric features of the workstation. A key factor in such layouts should be the spatial envelope needed by the crew to perform their duties. This begins with definition of a nominal work space posture and a nominal position of the body. Figure 33 illustrates major steps in this process.

Although these layouts can be prepared with pencil and paper, they are made more rapidly with computer-generated models having known link lengths and readily movable parts defined in a hierarchically constrained set of posturing instructions. Figure 33, originally prepared in the early 1970s, is generally correct, though I would now use different terminology for some of the links. For example, *terminal links* may be called *flesh links*, as they generally depict the thickness of fleshy material from the interjoint links to the surface of the body or clothing. Other details may change in accordance with the method of enfleshment of models and their scaling to match specific input dimensions. On the whole, the basic intent is to devise a starting point from which statistical variations and body movement needs can be developed.

Dimensional variations and body movements determine clearances and reaches. Step 6 also includes analyses of spatial needs for different sizes of crew and their motions during flight. Figure 34 depicts an example of worst-case conditions for knee clearance, an early graphical side-view layout to accommodate different sizes of leg segment lengths among the crew in the *Apollo* command module. In this simplified approach, the full range of hip joint locations and ankle joint locations is not shown. A more sophisticated

BASIC WORKSPACE LAYOUT & ANALYSIS USING ANTHROPOMETRIC DATA

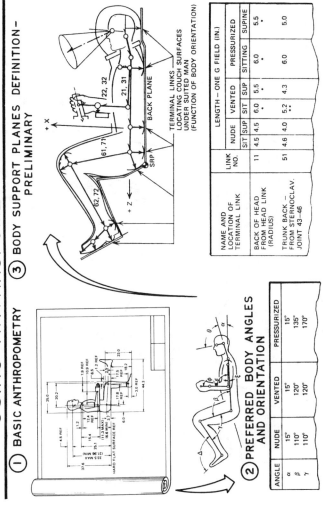

Figure 33. Design layout procedures for spacecraft couch (Roebuck et al., 1975).

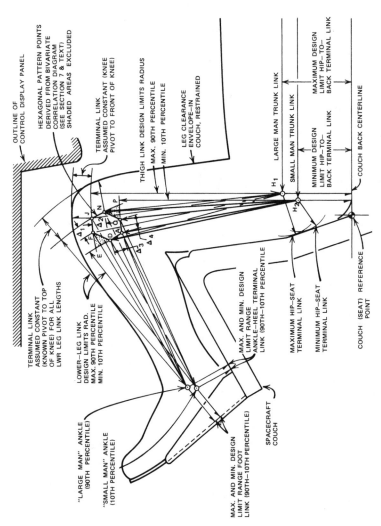

Figure 34. Development of design limits for knee location to determine clearance (Roebuck et al., 1975).

computer analysis today might suggest modifications, but such methods were not available at the time.

Other appropriate types of analysis include the determination of reachable areas on potential control panels, locations of eyes, and adjustments for couches. (Examples of reach envelopes will be shown later in relation to automotive interior design.) For the *Apollo* project, reachable areas were generated with paper and pencil. Computer modeling can make such analyses automatically and more quickly today.

Step 7. Mathematical Analysis

In Figure 31 (page 103), originally published in 1975, mathematical analysis by computer is shown as a separate step conducted in parallel with the drafting process. In the development days of the *Apollo* and space shuttle, computer analysis studies were performed in closed-off machine rooms using cumbersome punched card decks for input instructions and large, slow plotters. Such a separation of functions is much less common now, although many older design personnel prefer drafting with pencil on vellum and have not become comfortable with computers for design.

That situation notwithstanding, concurrent engineering approaches now being developed among technology leaders indicate that mathematical analysis by computer is the coming method of choice for nearly all engineering drafting functions. In light of this change, Steps 6 and 7 should be interchanged in Figure 31. Paper product outputs should now be considered "off to the side." Though not the main mode of analysis, they may still be a convenience for hand-carried presentations, they may be used as sketches to instruct CAD operators for design, and they are still valuable as backup documentation and for their lack of dependence on a computer for access.

Other, nongraphical mathematical analyses that may be needed to support design work include the estimation of new combinations of anthropometric dimensions, as I described in Chapter 5.

Step 8. Physical Small-Scale Model Analysis

As the 3D requirements are being developed in CAD or on drafting vellum, verification will often be desired in solid, 3D form. Small-scale models of the crew work space have been used to accomplish this preliminary visualization in an economical manner in the *Apollo*, space shuttle, and space station programs. In several cases, 2D and 3D models of the operators were constructed to aid the visualization process. These models were constructed of paper, paper-backed foam, corrugated cardboard, or even hardwoods. Additional options currently available are listed in Chapter 6.

Once constructed, models should be used in systematic evaluations. Procedures include physical measurements, placement of body models in working positions and postures, relocations of equipment, movement of seats, and so on. Photographic records of these situations are valuable for future reference and explanation of analyses. Results of these evaluations may lead directly to design decisions (Step 14) or to reevaluation of the CAD geometry or drawings.

Step 9. Preparation of Functional Test Requirements

Test or evaluation requirements must be formulated, either formally on paper or informally in the mind of the analyst. These evaluation activities may involve human subjects in mockups or computer model operators in CAD environments, depending on the complexity of judgments required and the stage of design. Evaluations are needed to verify design criteria or even to obtain original data on new relationships relating to environments, clothing effects, force and torque capabilities, visual obstructions, reach and clearance, fit, and function. These requirements include (1) how many and what sizes of test subjects are to be used in the evaluation, (2) what measurements are to be made, and (3) what instruments are needed or what support devices and personnel are required.

In the case of simulated space activities with subjects in pressurized suits, planning is complex and involves the commitment of extensive resources, some with long procurement cycles. Planning for evaluations often involves provisions for cutouts in a mockup for photography or video recording, air conditioning and pressurization equipment, plumbing for breathing gas, lighting, power sources, and safety provisions, and it may even include arranging for medical personnel and standby ambulances.

A key problem in ergonomic applications of anthropometric data is often deciding which standard, static body dimensions can be used directly and which must be ignored or greatly modified to accurately reflect real postures and support constraints, environmental conditions, and dynamic movements. For example, application tasks may call for highly restricted movement, as in inspecting a wing tank or working under a car. Specific restrictions often require data on diameters of the body that were not measured in standard anthropometric surveys. In some cases, solutions can be reached by estimations, but often, realistic solutions to application problems call for new measurements, usually on a few subjects, within short periods, and with limited funds.

Most project managers do not like to hear about requests to perform such "research"-oriented activity because they usually have not planned for it and they recognize that it could be costly and potentially result in delays in the completion of their milestones. Nonetheless, many issues of how to conduct human body measurements effectively — issues that were discussed earlier — may frequently come up and have to be dealt with, even though the original intent was simply to apply known data. Such contingencies need to be anticipated in planning design work and subsequent developments on products such as vehicles, furniture, factories, and buildings.

Step 10. Preparation of Mockups and Prototypes

These activities include not only the fabrication of the engineering design representations but also the construction and provisioning of special devices necessary to perform photography, measurements, and other engineering evaluations. For example, one of the early mockups of the *Apollo* command module was constructed in two halves that could be separated to obtain a view of the complete interior. Other mockups had removable sections, removable windows, plumbing for space suit air cooling and pressurization, transparent sections, and cutouts for suspension harnesses. Illustrations of various types of spacecraft and aircraft mockups are included in the book by Roebuck et al. (1975).

Step 11. Preparation of Reach and Clearance Envelopes

As evaluations of mockups take place with human subjects, parallel evaluations may begin with representations of movement envelopes, reach envelopes, or visual requirements. Figure 35 is an example of a 3D, full-scale, physical depiction (mockup) of a clearance envelope mounted in a vehicle mockup. The envelope shows the full range of helmeted head motion during the travel of shock struts caused by an emergency land impact (instead of a splashdown in the ocean, as planned) when the command module descends on parachutes in a 26-knot wind. The *Apollo* astronauts were supported on couches with shock absorbers that allowed a certain amount of movement to absorb much of the landing impact. This enabled them to move around quite a bit and in a complex manner within the small space of the command module, which meant that their heads might hit the sides or equipment attached to the wall during such landings.

The envelope that was developed showed designers that the crew members' heads were not likely to hit any of the hard inner structures under landing conditions. It also showed where potential spaces were available for the installation of new equipment in critical areas. This envelope so nearly filled the *Apollo* command module mockup that it had to be fabricated in three pieces that were bolted together after insertion into the mockup.

Although computer analyses were performed to develop and verify the motions of the bodies and couches, computing power at that time was limited, and the output was plotted on large paper sheets with ink pens. Today, the geometry of clearance envelopes can be readily input in a CAD representation of 3D work/occupancy sites, with substantial savings in fabrication, handling, materials procurement, storage, safety of subjects, and possibly much hard physical labor. Furthermore, the resulting 3D representation can be easily viewed from many different points merely by twisting dials or punching buttons.

Figure 35. Envelope of clearance needed for Apollo *crew and couch during hard landing (courtesy of Space Division, Rockwell International Corporation).*

Step 12. Preparation of Special Gauges and Measuring Devices

Frequently, new and unusual devices may be needed for a special workplace evaluation. Figure 36 is an example of a device for positioning crew members in the correct position for docking operations.

Step 13. Mockup and Prototype Evaluation

Results of evaluations of mockups or of prototypes with real subjects may be used to revise work space drawings (Step 6) or design criteria (Step 14). These evaluations require arrangements for the evaluation of subjects, procurement of test apparatus, scheduling of evaluations, procurement of recording and photographic services, actual performance of the evaluations and recording of data, followed by data reduction, analysis, and reporting. In the spacecraft development cycle, these activities included static mockup evaluations, evaluations of mockups and laboratory gear in aircraft to simulate weightlessness for a short time, underwater simulations for long-term simulation of weightlessness, simulations of launch and re-entry activities in centrifuges, and water surface recovery operations.

Mockup evaluations should be arranged and performed to answer the question, "What kind of information would I need to prepare a three-view, orthographic drawing or a 3D CAD geometric definition of the work space and operator?" At a minimum, evaluations should include definitions of reach, clearance, interference, adjustments, and visual obstructions. Sketches and photographs of the mockup and critical postures help to explain the dimensions measured.

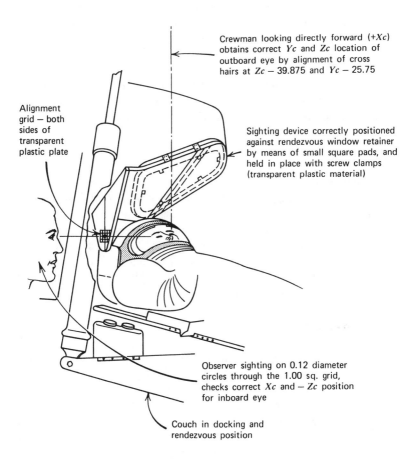

Figure 36. Special anthropometric measurement and gauging device for use in mockup (courtesy of Space Division, Rockwell International Corporation).

Step 14. Preparation of Design Letters, Memoranda, Standards, and Specifications

The major output from the foregoing series of activities is in the form of advice. Such advice is usually transmitted in the form of written or spoken requirements or recommendations. In some cases, video records or motion picture film may be used, but their expense tends to preclude their extensive use. Letters and memoranda, together with graphical and tabular enclosures, generally constitute the primary end product of all of the steps in the process, the reading and interpretation of data, statistical analyses and syntheses, mockup evaluations, and sketching and drawing. Work space design recommendations may be also documented formally as design standards, "interface control documents," and specifications for work space design.

In the real world, not all advice is accepted, even if it has been obtained at great cost.

> **To be convincing, letters and other documents of advice and requirements should be accompanied by clear explanations of the meaning and expected consequences of proper use, misuse, or no use of the advice.**

As for all human factors specialists, it is also important to build a reputation for accuracy, sound judgment, and acceptance by peers in your field of expertise and by associates in engineering departments.

The detailed steps and interrelationships discussed in the foregoing presentation are represented in part or whole in many other development projects. The vocabulary may differ and the environments almost surely will be different, but the general functions are recognizable. Some key differences and similarities are pointed out in the next section.

Airplane Cockpits

Much of the preceding description of design steps is directly applicable to the design of aircraft cockpits, given that the steps were a product of the aircraft industry. However, in most aircraft, the environments are often more benign and earthlike than is the case with spacecraft. Weightlessness is experienced only in acrobatics or unexpected down draft conditions. Pressure suits are generally worn only by pilots in combat aircraft or in noncombat flying under rare experimental flight conditions.

Still, aircraft engineering has pioneered methods for the application of anthropometry that are not only interesting in themselves but have potential applicability to the design of many other vehicular and stationary work spaces. Again, as the following discussion unfolds, think of each particular example as an illustration of potentially general methodology.

Design Specification Layouts

Aircraft design has evolved more slowly than spacecraft and has a longer history. As a result, some important key geometrical guidelines have been developed for different types of aircraft. Figure 37 is one example, applicable to a fighter aircraft cockpit of the 1960s.

As a starting point, this design standard is useful for many situations, as long as it is not used uncritically. In particular, we would expect that many dimensions would change to account for different population characteristics, different clothing, and different mission requirements. In fact, changes often occur before specifications can be prepared by government agencies to reflect them. As a result, the current trend is to specify the desired crew performance rather than simply to specify finite dimensions of cockpits. The aircraft contractor, therefore, should prepare specification drawings based on current and forecast pilot sizes, vehicle mission profiles, and planned control systems. For example, it is not relevant to specify torques for joystick control travel if a side stick or trackball is to be used.

Even so, the concept of devising a "skeleton" layout at the start of a project has value as a benchmark for the systematic analysis of key dimensional needs. Using computer models, you could determine the percentage of a population accommodated by such a cockpit geometry and then develop overall envelopes for reach, clearance, and adjustments that accommodate different percentages of potential crew members. As modifications are made to population statistics, posture requirements, or vision parameters, the process could be iterated to determine the potential benefits of the design changes proposed.

Clearance Envelopes

A drawing of the side view of a clearance envelope for a fighter aircraft is shown in Figure 38. The envelope accounts for head and limb motions of various types. Envelopes can be the basis for the development of minimal volume requirements for aircraft crew compartments — data that are useful in early stages of preliminary design.

Adjustment Envelopes

The typical aircraft pilot seat for passenger airliners or multiengine bombers is adjustable in fore-aft and up-down directions and sometimes sideways. In addition, back angles, armrests, seat pan angles, and lumbar supports may be adjustable. The vertical and fore-aft adjustments are

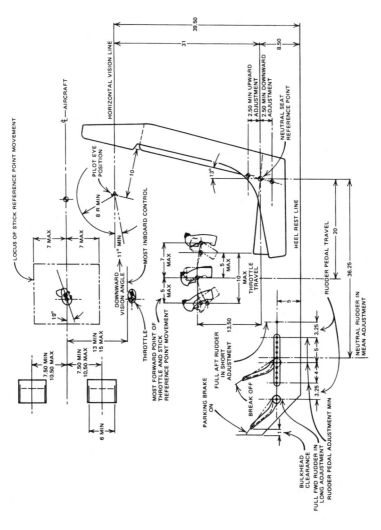

Figure 37. Typical standard design guide for dimensions of military cockpit with ejection seat (U.S. Air Force, 1968).

required so that pilots can place their eyes correctly to see upward and downward and to enable them to reach pedals and manual controls. Requirements for these ranges of adjustment involve many complex anthropometric relationships, particularly regressions between eye height and body posture, leg and arm length, effects of clothing and equipment, and task demands. A picture or set of numbers that defines these possible adjustments is critical to the successful design of the seat and its integration with the piloting functions of the craft.

Figure 38 provides a simple example, limited to vertical adjustment along a rail that slants 13 degrees aft at the top to assist clearance during ejection.

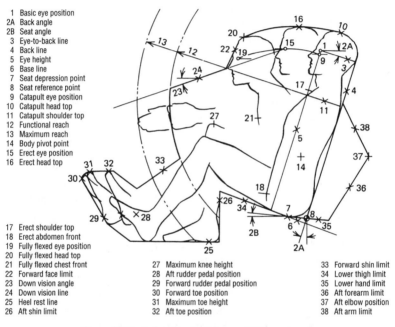

1	Basic eye position
2A	Back angle
2B	Seat angle
3	Eye-to-back line
4	Back line
5	Eye height
6	Base line
7	Seat depression point
8	Seat reference point
9	Catapult eye position
10	Catapult head top
11	Catapult shoulder top
12	Functional reach
13	Maximum reach
14	Body pivot point
15	Erect eye position
16	Erect head top
17	Erect shoulder top
18	Erect abdomen front
19	Fully flexed eye position
20	Fully flexed head top
21	Fully flexed chest front
22	Forward face limit
23	Down vision angle
24	Down vision line
25	Heel rest line
26	Aft shin limit
27	Maximum knee height
28	Aft rudder pedal position
29	Forward rudder pedal position
30	Forward toe position
31	Maximum toe height
32	Aft toe position
33	Forward shin limit
34	Lower thigh limit
35	Lower hand limit
36	Aft forearm limit
37	Aft elbow position
38	Aft arm limit

Figure 38. Basic functional envelope — military aircraft (courtesy of McDonnell Douglas Corporation).

Aircraft Passenger Accommodations

Several design issues for passenger aircraft are similar to those for buses, trains, and other mass transit vehicles and for auditorium seating.

Shin Clearance for Seating

Leg clearance is an important consideration in any set of seats arranged in rows. The economics that drive such designs favor close front-to-back spacing to accommodate more people in a given space. Anthropometric problems involve the determination of clearances for entry and exit and the angles and contours that ensure comfort for various common postures during long-term occupancy.

Figure 39 illustrates a graphical method for determining the percentage of persons accommodated in various leg postures. Note that the solution does not simply relate to the 95th percentile man but considers a wide variety of combinations of two leg dimensions. Computer models can determine the percentage accommodated by analysis of collisions between the human model and seat structure.

Shoulder Clearance for Seating

The lateral spacing of seats is also important in passenger aircraft, buses, auditoria, and other groups of seats. Figure 40 illustrates the results of an extensive study of how wide seats should be to accommodate three passengers sitting side by side.

Three different criteria were used for this study. One assumed that the people were centered on their own seats and did not overlap adjacent seats. Another assumed that they were shoulder to shoulder (bench criterion). Finally, the people were assumed to be centered in their seats but could overlap shoulders, such that when large men sat next to small women, both could still sit at the centerline of their seats without interference. Note that this figure is based on results for a population measured in the early 1940s (Hooton, 1945). Historical growth of Americans during the nearly five decades following these measurements makes such data obsolete for current design.

Design of Lavatories for People with Handicaps

Current federal regulations require that wide-bodied aircraft provide at least one lavatory that can accommodate people who require wheelchairs for mobility. A study of needs was sponsored by the Paralyzed Veterans of America, National Easter Seal Society, National Multiple Sclerosis Society, and United Cerebral Palsy Association. The results were reported in a document that provides guidelines for such designs (Warren and Valois, 1991). The information was then used in developing model guidelines for accessible lavatories in twin-aisle aircraft (Ad Hoc Working Group on Design Guidelines, 1991). As part of the study, a criterion of assistance for 95th percentile males (as defined by Diffrient et al., 1974, in Humanscale 1/2/3) was employed. Figure 41 illustrates the key design dimensions and a plan view of the space needed by a 97.5 percentile male for lateral transfer movement from a wheelchair by an assisting attendant who is also a 97.5 percentile male.

Figure 42 shows the space needed for the same two sizes of persons to accomplish a 90-degree transfer. Two potential positions for the assistant are

Leg clearance determination

1. Determine graded series of leg positions for study.

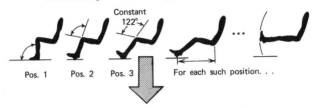

Pos. 1   Pos. 2   Pos. 3   For each such position. . .

2. Layout allowable variations of leg component lengths in given space.

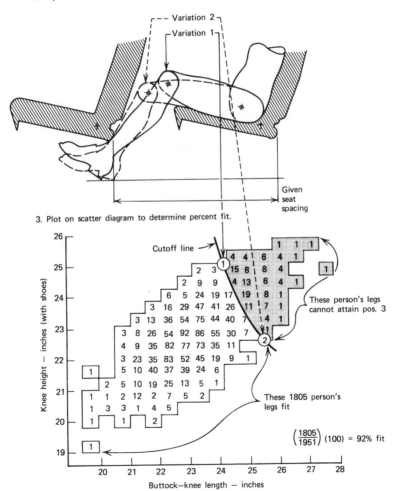

3. Plot on scatter diagram to determine percent fit.

$$\left(\frac{1805}{1951}\right)(100) = 92\% \text{ fit}$$

Figure 39. Shin clearance analysis method (Roebuck, 1957).

indicated (pivot points A and B). These illustrations are indicative of personal accommodations that will be figuring strongly in new designs for buildings and vehicles as well as aircraft over the next few years. Architects must include provisions to accommodate wheelchairs that are larger than the minimal-width types used in aircraft, and perhaps to accommodate other methods for patient transfer. However, the basic anthropometric considerations indicated above will be among those needed for the design of many kinds of facilities. For additional requirements for access by people with handicaps, consult compliance manuals prepared for the Americans with Disabilities Act (Schneid, 1993).

Automotive Vehicle Interiors

The design of personal, commercial, and military automobiles involves many of the same anthropometric considerations that are involved in the design of aircraft cockpit and passenger seating space. However, there are significant and interesting differences in the type and range of the population accommodated, the fixed points selected for geometric reference, and the approaches to protection of the user from environmental conditions.

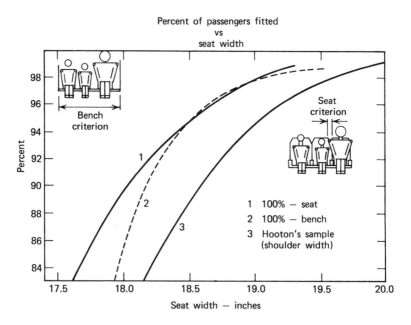

Figure 40. Results of an analysis of seat widths for three-abreast combinations (Lippert, 1958).

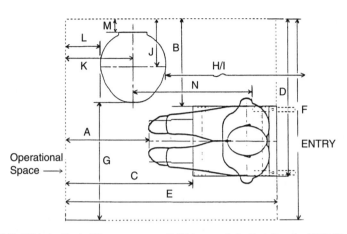

A. Wall to W/C footrest front = 19″
B. Wall to W/C = 20″
C. Wall to W/C front wheel = 29″
D. Wall to W/C side = 36″
E. Wall to W/C back = 48″ (w/c handles folded in)
F. Width required for transfer activities = 46″
G. Toilet front to wall opposite = 27″

H. Maximum reach shoulder to fingertip = 30″ 97.5% male
I. Maximum reach shoulder to fingertip = 24.7″ 2.5% female
J. Toilet center from wall behind = 11″
K. Toilet center from side wall = 15.5″
L. Toilet edge to side wall = 8″
M. Toilet edge to back wall = 3″
N. Transfer radius for 97.5% male = 27″

ASSUMPTIONS: Person in W/C – 19″W × 29″L (97.5% male dimensions)
Able Bodied Squatting – 19″W × 26″ (97.5% male dimensions)
Toilet Seat – 15″W × 16″L

Figure 41. Plan view of space requirements for a lavatory for disabled persons (courtesy of Paralyzed Veterans of America, National Easter Seal Society, National Multiple Sclerosis Society, and United Cerebral Palsy Association).

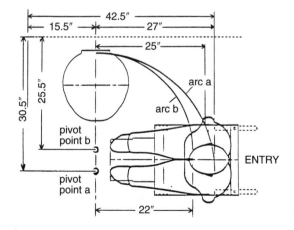

Figure 42. Plan view of space requirements for a lavatory for disabled persons — arc of motion (courtesy of Paralyzed Veterans of America, National Easter Seal Society, National Multiple Sclerosis Society, and United Cerebral Palsy Association).

Definition and Description of the User Population

Some significant anthropometric descriptors, based on studies of drivers of automobiles, buses, and trucks in the United States, are briefly summarized in Table 4. Also listed there are related effects on the design of automobile interiors and references to where more data can be obtained. Note that truck drivers, as an occupational subpopulation, have been studied more thoroughly than any other group of civilian drivers. For private passenger automobiles, the description of the driving population has been based for many years on the anthropometric data collected as part of the health examination survey (often abbreviated HES) conducted during 1960–1962 by the U.S. Health, Education and Welfare Department (now the Department of Health and Human Services). Several reports on the anthropometry of the study were prepared (e.g., Stoudt, Damon, McFarland, and Roberts, 1965). Also, the most useful data on means, standard deviations, and percentiles appear in NASA Reference Publication 1024 (Anthropology Research Project staff, 1978b) and Appendix C of this book.

Appendix C also includes coefficients of correlation for these civilian dimensions, as published by Churchill et al. (1977). However, the age of these data makes the current status of the anthropometry of the driving public highly suspect. Studies of civilian health in 1971–1974 (Abraham, Johnson, and Najjar, 1979) and 1976–1980 (Najjar and Rowland, 1987) have included few dimensions, but those few suggest that the height of civilians has increased. They also confirm that weight variations among civilians are much greater than those of military populations. Nevertheless, the data from the 1988 survey of the U.S. Army (Gordon et al., 1989a, 1989b; Cheverud et al., 1990a, 1990b, 1990c, 1990d) may be the closest available to a current description of the anthropometry of U.S. citizens, even though they are biased by selection standards for military service and have a much smaller age range.

I judge the means of the military data to match civilian dimensions today within plus or minus 1% for Stature and Weight and probably within plus or minus 3% for most heights and long-bone lengths. However, standard deviations and skewness of the distributions for weight and related fleshy diameters and circumferences of Army personnel are very likely smaller than for the general public. The most generally useful of the extensive series of reports on the Army anthropometry survey of 1988 are listed in Chapter 6, Table 3 (see page 83).

As compared with aircraft and spacecraft design, automotive design has undergone a relatively slow evolution over many model changes. This has permitted the Society of Automotive Engineers (SAE) in the United States to develop a greater degree of standardization than has been possible in the more volatile aerospace industry. Devices that are developed to incorporate and represent the accumulated experience of work space designers can be used many

TABLE 4
Population Characteristics and Design Considerations of Automotive Drivers and Passengers

Population Name and Selection Characteristics	Other Population Descriptors	Samples Investigated	References and Sampling Area, Dates	Significant Design Considerations
Drivers				
General: age 15–75 years; male and female; average health and whole-bodied	Wide range of income, education, race, age, body build, strength	18–79 years, 6672 persons represent U.S. population 524 females, 509 males represent U.S. driver population	Stoudt et al. (1965); U.S. 1959–1962 Stoudt, Crowley et al. (1970): U.S.	Wide design range for adjustment of seat, other controls if desirable. Some selection by model size.
Bus and truck: primarily male; healthy, whole-bodied	Stockier, more mesomorphic, less gynandromorphic than average American male, bigger in weight, breadths, girth but not height	272 civilian bus and truck drivers. 103 were champions, "roadeo" competitors	Damon and McFarland (1955); U.S.	Design truck cabs for large sizes of men. Consider improved controls if smaller, weaker men or females needed as drivers
Champions	Taller, broader shoulders, longer forearms than average			
Military	Smaller, younger than other soldiers	Military truck drivers	See also Damon, Stoudt, and McFarland (1966); U.S.	
Orthopedically handicapped; male and female, limb or limbs missing	See reference	See reference	McFarland et al. (1968); U.S.	Design special controls as required for handicap prosthesis form/capability (e.g., power boosting brakes, steering)
Pregnant women, age 15–45 years (Also need special attention as passengers)	Average 8 years younger, 13 lb heavier than average females, abdominal depth 2 in greater than other women measured	203 healthy women (in third to ninth month), Boston, Massachusetts	Stoudt, Crowley et al. (1970); U.S.	Special assistance for ingress/egress, fit behind wheel; Special protection against impact injury in crash; Adjustability for controls to assist reach
Passengers				
Infants and children, age 0–15 years, male/female	Body proportions different from adults, relatively high center of mass (top heavy).	82 child occupants in auto collisions	Siegel, Nahum, Appleby (1968)	Special attention in auxiliary seats and restraints for impact protection, consider relatively higher center of mass, potential injury from more fragile auxiliary seat structure
		Accident studies	Burdi et al. (1969); Snyder (1970a)	
Elderly persons	See references	65–79 years	Stoudt et al. (1965); U.S. 1959–1962	
		133 Spanish-American war veterans	Damon and Stoudt (1963)	

Source: Roebuck et al. (1975)

125

times by different companies for evaluation of similarly shaped work spaces. Notable examples of such devices are the SAE standard H-point machine (to be described) and the related 2D articulated drafting template manikin.

Body Posture Selection

This is depicted in Step 6.1 of Figure 31 (see page 103). Although some delivery vehicles and street cars provide for standing operators, the majority of cars, buses, trucks, and off-road farm vehicles require the seated posture. The operator's work involves normal driving tasks, such as rotating the steering wheel, reaching for and operating controls, and looking out of windows and at mirrors.

Orthopedically handicapped drivers introduce variabilities into the body positioning requirements, including different controls, such as hand-operated controls in place of foot controls (Breaking New Ground Resource Center, 1986). People with disabilities may be considered a new population that should be provided with rearrangements of controls, perhaps power-assisted brakes and steering. If so accommodated, they can be quite capable of handling vehicles (Breaking New Ground Resource Center, 1986).

As in the case of passenger aircraft seating, comfort is a significant design criterion for automobile passengers and drivers. Changes have gradually been made in lumbar supports for seats that improve the driver's posture. Although these changes may increase comfort and health for seating, any single, fixed body position or seat profile — even if very comfortable in the beginning — becomes increasingly uncomfortable after long, uninterrupted sitting. A variety of postures and pressure distributions is necessary.

Anthropometry affects not only the previously discussed aspects of seating in a well-supported attitude but also the driver's ability to drive a car or other vehicle with ease. Human mass properties and vibration resonances become involved as designers consider isolation from road impacts, mechanical vibrations, noises, and uncomfortable temperatures. Comfort has become a recognized factor in such utilitarian vehicles as modern farm tractors. Some of these have been fitted with fully enclosed, air-conditioned cabs and even stereo music systems as well as upholstered and adjustable seats. Such features affect body postures and application of anthropometric design data.

Foot Location: Package Origin Point

In contrast to aircraft cockpit "design eye" or "seat reference" points, current automobile work space layout in the United States usually begins with the location of the accelerator pedal as the reference point. This is possible because of the large expanse of windshield and relative unimportance of downward vision over the hood. This reference point has been variously called the *heel hard point* or *accelerator heel point* (AHP) or *pedal geometry origin*

(PGO). The AHP is defined as the actual point of contact of the heel on the floor. The PGO is located at the same fore-aft station but is at the centerline (sagittal plane) of the driver's seat. Currently, heel points are used mainly for truck design; for passenger cars, the ball of the foot is more often used as a reference point. The layout drawing (often made at full scale) defining the body, seat, and compartment space is called a *package drawing* or layout.

Seat Reference Points

The reference point used in automobile design until 1961 was the *A point*. This was located 5 in forward of the nondepressed seat back on the surface of the cushion. However, because automobile seat cushions provide a wide variety of depression under load, this proved to be an unreliable point for comparing available interior space and reach between different types of cars.

To circumvent this difficulty, the Society of Automotive Engineers developed the concept of the *H point*, a point that is intended to approximate the mean of the distribution of hip joint centers for the population of seat occupants (drivers and passengers). By definition, it is located in a particular seat by use of a standard, 3D partial manikin called the *H-point machine*.

The H-Point Machine and Drafting Template

The SAE J826a (Society of Automotive Engineers, 1990) 3D partial manikin illustrated in Figure 43 uses the weight and body contour of the mythical 50th percentile male, presumably of the U.S. driving public. The main parts of the manikins are one trunk and pelvis section, two thighs, two calves, and two foot sections. The leg segments are adjustable to different percentile lengths. Simple, one-degree-of-freedom hinges allow for some movement.

For preliminary design, a 2D articulated drafting manikin representation of the H-point machine is used to establish approximate leg clearances using 90th or 95th percentile leg segments. Figure 44 illustrates this manikin.

In concept (50th percentile male) and realization, both 2D and 3D H-point manikins have limitations as representations of human beings. However, simplicity in design furthers the use of these phantoms for standardization of the H point and for gross evaluation of the leg clearances of the operator or passenger. Attempts to improve the manikins and the procedures are continuing through the SAE's Design Devices Subcommittee of the Human Factors Engineering Committee. Modeling methods described in SAE standards J1516 and J1517 are being employed as part of this effort (Manary, Schneider, Flannagan, and Eby, 1994). For further information, write to SAE (400 Commonwealth Drive, Warrendale, PA 15096-0001 USA).

The seat range of adjustment and reference location is defined (in terms of the H point) with respect to the vehicle reference point (AHP, PGO, or ball

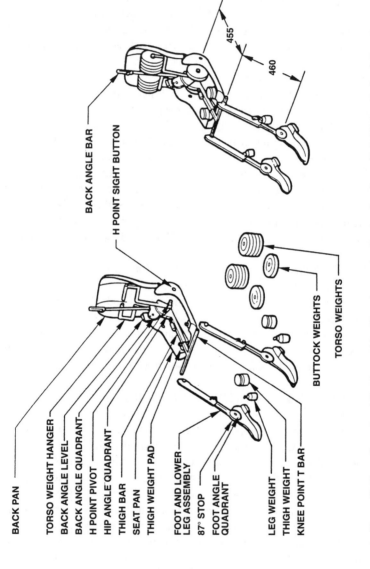

BACK PAN

TORSO WEIGHT HANGER

BACK ANGLE LEVEL

BACK ANGLE QUADRANT

H POINT PIVOT

HIP ANGLE QUADRANT

THIGH BAR

SEAT PAN

THIGH WEIGHT PAD

FOOT AND LOWER LEG ASSEMBLY

87° STOP

FOOT ANGLE QUADRANT

LEG WEIGHT

THIGH WEIGHT

KNEE POINT T BAR

BACK ANGLE BAR

H POINT SIGHT BUTTON

455

460

BUTTOCK WEIGHTS

TORSO WEIGHTS

Figure 43. Three-dimensional H-point machine (from Automotive Ergonomics, figure 11, R. W. Roe, Taylor & Francis, Bristol, PA. Reproduced with permission. All rights reserved).

128

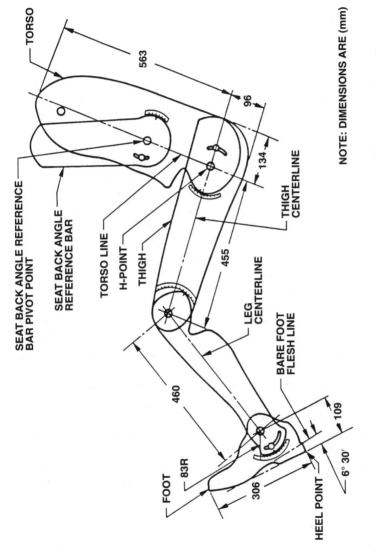

NOTE: DIMENSIONS ARE (mm)

SEAT BACK ANGLE REFERENCE BAR PIVOT POINT

SEAT BACK ANGLE REFERENCE BAR

TORSO LINE

H-POINT

THIGH

LEG CENTERLINE

BARE FOOT FLESH LINE

FOOT

HEEL POINT

TORSO

THIGH CENTERLINE

563

96

134

455

460

83R

109

6° 30'

306

Figure 44. Two-dimensional H-point manikin (from Automotive Ergonomics, figure 11, R. W. Roe, Taylor & Francis, Bristol, PA. Reproduced with permission. All rights reserved).

129

of foot). For example, a medium passenger car for the general U.S. public may have a fore-aft seat adjustment range of 6 in. along a slanted plane dropping 2 in. as it traverses from front to back. Designs such as this are intended to permit all drivers (within a selected percentile range, such as 5th percentile female to 95th percentile male) to reach the accelerator pedal, the steering wheel, and other controls comfortably. Drivers also have to be able to see enough of the roadway to drive safely. In the case of older and smaller female drivers, it is questionable if this seat adjustment range is adequate. This issue reflects on the definition of the user population and the designer's responsibility to provide adequate adjustments for a wide range of drivers. Demographic changes caused by increased longevity result in an increasing number of older (and shorter) drivers.

When selecting seat adjustment ranges, keep in mind that long legs are not necessarily indicative of long trunks (or long Eye Height, Sitting). Therefore, adjustability of the seat pan height should be independent of the fore-aft adjustment to maintain equivalent vision and head clearance. However, the commonly used, simple rearward declined seat adjustment is often feasible largely because of the wide allowances in eye height permitted by automotive window design and loose standards for forward visibility. The small range of vertical adjustment effectively controls the worst-case variations in head clearance from the interior ceiling.

The next step involving the H-point machine is often to build a 3D mockup of the driver and passenger compartment (Step 10 of Figure 31 on page 103; see Kyropoulos and Roe, 1968). This mockup is called a *seating buck*. Although the seating buck is simply constructed of wood or foam with some metal fittings, the seat is fully sprung and trimmed (covered with fabric).

The 3D manikin is then placed on the seat using carefully defined procedures. Because of its weight, it sinks into the seat pan and back, establishing the H point for further layout analysis. If the designer is satisfied with the appearance of the seating buck, more elaborate mockups are constructed and tested with human subjects until the final design is tested in an actual vehicle. Additional mockup tests can establish envelopes of clearance with respect to the defined H point and heel point references. From these, seat adjustment requirements may also be developed.

Eye Position Standards

Depending on limits of steering wheel clearance and reach, heel reach, vision requirements, seat adjustments, fore-aft eye position distribution, and sitting eye height distribution in a relaxed, comfortable body posture, a point between the driver's eyes will not be at a single point in the car. Rather, it will be located within a roughly elliptical space (as seen from the side). To determine the size of that ellipse, a joint measurement effort was organized by the automobile industry (Meldrum, 1965). Some 2300 people, primarily visitors at an exhibition, were seated in either a Ford, Plymouth, or Chevrolet convertible. Two cameras set at 90 degrees took pictures of each subject. Eye positions were calculated from the photographs, and subsequent analyses of the photographs were incorporated into SAE recommended practice J941a (Society of Automotive Engineers, 1967). J941a shows Driver's Eye Range contours weighted for equal numbers of females and males in the population. As with many such studies, changes have gradually been introduced over the years.

The contours (elliptical by definition) of the eye range distribution depict perimeters of envelopes in plan and side view that encompass selected ranges of accommodation (e.g., 95 percent accommodation). They are referred to by the coined name, *eyellipses*. Tangent lines drawn to these contours represent lines of sight such that at least those selected percentages of eyes are located toward the midpoint side of the line. The tangents provide a conservative estimate because some locations of eyes are outside the ellipses but still not outside the sight lines.

Later studies have provided methods of accounting for viewing targets located at extreme lateral angles, including limited head and eye movements (Devlin and Roe, 1968), and accounting for changes in the eyellipse locations brought about by changes in body posture at different seat body angles (Roe and Hammond, 1972).

A number of prepared templates can be used to locate the eyellipses at different seat angles. The H point serves as the reference point in this technique. These templates are applicable to passenger cars, trucks, and buses with bench or bucket seats. The procedures recommended and the eyellipses are described in detail in SAE J941c (Society of Automotive Engineers, 1990). These same basic concepts are applicable to any work space design not dictated by a fixed eye reference point. Of course, the contours will be different, given that they are not based on conditions existing in the auto exhibition where they were measured and in the three vehicles, manufactured in 1963, that were used in these measurements. For example, current auto seats have a lumbar support that is firmer than those of earlier automobiles and tend to move a driver's trunk to a more upright posture, thus changing the eye positions.

Reach Envelopes

The critical reach dimensions for automotive design involve the forward reach areas around the steering wheel — to the dashboard, from the side wall across to the center of the vehicle, and perhaps across to the usual place for the map and glove storage compartment in front of the front seat passenger. The introduction of shoulder restraint harness systems in the 1960s, mandated by government regulation, created a significant new need for reach data. With the heel reference point being at one extreme of the human body and the fingers at another extreme of the body link-joint system, the relation of the heel point to the sweep of the fingers is difficult to determine. The range of motion of the fingers can be conceived as a 3D envelope. However, you must consider a large number of combinations of body dimensions to derive the contours of such envelopes for large populations.

One response to these complexities was to develop special automotive design standards using measurement techniques and representative subject samples in mockups (Steps 10 through 13 of Figure 31, page 103). The approach was to take measurements on a sample of drivers seated in car mockups using the accelerator heel point for reference. In an article describing such a study, Chaffee (1969) pointed out that the envelope of reach must represent a given percentile of reach capability of the sample population, not the reach capability of a mythical 50th percentile man or woman or even of a 5th percentile man or woman. That concept has been accepted by many in the road vehicle industry today and described in articles on how to evaluate vehicle accommodations (Philippart and Kuchenmeister, 1985; Philippart, Roe, Arnold, and Kuchenmeister, 1984; Roe, 1993). Roe (1993) refers to it as a *task-oriented percentile model*, in contrast to the *manikin-oriented model*, which uses manikins with many common percentile dimensions. It is another approach to the development of accommodation percentages that are the basis of the previously described Crewstation Assessment of Reach computer program (see Monte Carlo generation, Chapter 6) for aircraft cockpit seat reach analysis (Harris et al., 1980).

Various methods have been used to develop reach envelopes of human subjects in mockups. For example, Chaffee (1969) advocated the selection of radial reach directions from a midpoint between the shoulders of seated drivers. He called this point the *ergosphere origin*. Chaffee used a mockup arrangement for reach measurements that had specific features common to most automobiles, a policy that has been followed by many others in the automotive field (Roe, 1993). These features included typical controls, seat belt and shoulder restraint harness, and typical seat upholstery and seat orientations.

For defining reach points in space, Chaffee used a 9-ft-square panel located at various distances in front of the subject and a similar set of positions to the side. The forward reach panels were cut out to accommodate the subject's legs. The subject's task was to use the left hand to position a 1-in.-diameter knob as far out as possible along each of 15 numbered radial lines on the panel. Ergosphere origin points were then determined from those radial plan traces. This resulted in a different EO for forward reach and side-ward reach ergospheres.

Subsequent reach studies have generally opted for alternative measurement devices. For example, I had been involved in planning for a study of the anthropometry and reach capability of truck drivers. In that study, the reach limits were determined by adjustable horizontal rods placed in front of the subject in a mockup. The entire mockup was constructed inside the cargo compartment of a truck and driven to several sites around the United States (Sanders, 1977). A similar study was conducted in the early 1980s (Sanders and Shaw, 1985).

The current standard SAE Control Reach Measuring Fixture uses push rods mounted on a vertical plate that can be moved laterally (Roe, 1993). It is essentially an abbreviated mockup fitted with a seat, wheel, and accelerator pedal, as illustrated in Figure 45 (Roe, 1993). The resulting data yield curves in horizontal and vertical planes arranged parallel to the car's longitudinal axis (Figure 46).

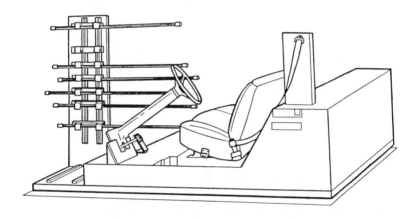

Figure 45. SAE fixture for measuring control reach (from Automotive Ergonomics, *figure 11, R. W. Roe, Taylor & Francis, Bristol, PA. Reproduced with permission. All rights reserved).*

Human and Cabin Dimensions

The dimensions of large people determine many of the overall space dimensions of automobile interiors, particularly overall height and length of the space. However, the dimensions of small people cannot be ignored because they are related to reach and location of the steering wheel. Allowances for entry and exit, vibration, road-induced jostling, impacts, clothing, and hair styling must be added to the static, nude dimensions for the driver and passenger. In almost all cases, these allowances require that an increase in the volume be allocated to the persons in the vehicles. Clothing, conversely, may reduce arm mobility and thus reduce reach capability.

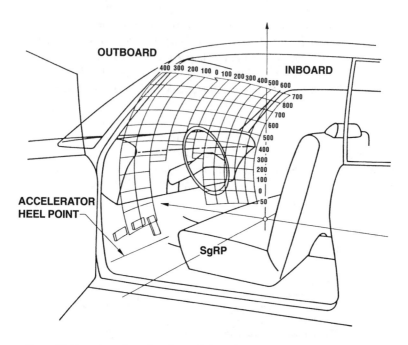

Figure 46. Control reach envelope in a vehicle work space (from Automotive Ergonomics, *figure 11, R. W. Roe, Taylor & Francis, Bristol, PA. Reproduced with permission. All rights reserved).*

Restraints such as shoulder harnesses and lap belts may further reduce reach and limit other dynamic body movements.

Child restraint seats also should be considered for design purposes. Earlier models were shown by Snyder (1970b) to offer little or no protection to the occupant. In contrast to adults, a child should not be restrained at the shoulder level while its head is free to move: the relatively large mass of the head can snap forward on the restrained torso, resulting in serious neurological injury. Compared with that of adults, the cervical structure of the child's neck is rather weak (in fact, it is one of the weaker parts of the adult human body). Net or webbing systems or air bags that catch the child would be better because they distribute the impact over larger areas of the elastic and fragile body.

Snyder proposed a "capsule" protection system (offering protection from side impacts also) for both adults and children. Snyder's reports on human impact tolerance (1970a, 1970b) described restraint systems in land, air, and space vehicles. He gave an excellent overview of the state of the art and on future concepts and design directions. Over the years, before and since Snyder's reports, related articles have frequently appeared in the proceedings of the Stapp Car Crash Conferences (e.g., Rogers and Silver, 1968; Severy, Brink, and Baird, 1968; Siegel, Nahum, and Appleby, 1968).

Many design requirement interactions occur and complicate the design problem. Engineering practicality, economics, and schedules force the anthropometrist to make a careful determination of which dimensions are really critical. Roebuck et al. (1975) summarized recommendations by several authors. More recently, Roe (1993) illustrated some of the important dimensions that define interior space and access (Figure 47).

Applications of Mathematical and Physical Analogs of the Human Body

Models of the human body (both 3D articulated dummies and mathematical analogs) play an important role in automobile design, particularly as regards crash safety. For example, physical dummies are used in studies of crash safety for automobiles. It is likely that more testing with more sizes and types of dummies is now conducted in the automotive industry than in the aerospace industry. These models represent the hard and soft tissues of the human body and its biomechanical behavior in various force environments. Mathematical computer models for crash investigation have evolved over many years since the early models developed at Cornell University and Calspan (McHenry and Naab, 1966). These models have been given different titles for various different applications, such as crash victim simulation (CVS; see Fleck, Butler, and Vogel, 1975) and articulated total body model, or ATB (Obergefell, Gardner, Kaleps, and Fleck, 1988).

Recent studies by researchers for the University of Michigan Transportation Research Institute and Michigan State University have attempted to model human skeletal positions and orientations of drivers by computer mathematical models (Boughner, 1991; Haas, 1989). These applications have been primarily concerned with questions of comfort. Current practice in automotive design also favors computer graphics modeling over use of the 2D H-point manikin for drafting. The use of these manikins may be completely phased out in a few years.

Furniture for Computer Workstations

The design of computer workstations is among the most recent topics to be studied by human factors specialists, and it may now be the most popular, judging from the large number of articles and books that deal with the subject in some way. A considerable number of studies and experiments have been performed on various aspects of the computer workstation, but only a few dealing with anthropometrics will be touched on here.

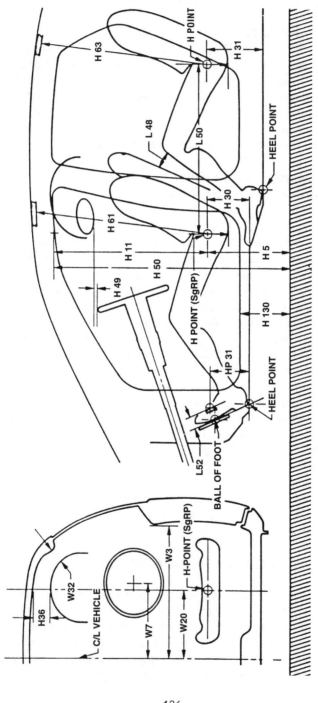

Figure 47. Some dimensions in SAE J1100 that define interior space and access (from Automotive Ergonomics, figure 11, R. W. Roe, Taylor & Francis, Bristol, PA. Reproduced with permission. All rights reserved).

Population Definition

Although furniture of many kinds has been used for thousands of years, it has not always been designed according to the latest understanding of anthropometric dimensions. This lamentable situation applies also to computer workstation furniture, according to Kleeman (1987). He wrote, "Furniture dimensions have traditionally been based on habit and tradition; very seldom is anthropometry used in furniture design" (p. 4). Although Kleeman cited several sources of "good information," he also indicated that the data have drawbacks, particularly because of the small size of some samples and the fact that many do not contain recent data.

Kleeman further suggested that the secular changes in some populations (e.g., U.S. Air Force males) may require a shift to a wider diversity in sizes in recent times. His main theme, with which I concur, is that you should carefully decide on the criteria for anthropometric design standards. Designers should not be stampeded into using the 5th and 95th percentiles as criteria for civilian furniture, even though these are the customary values used in the design of military combat aircraft or spacecraft. Kleeman's approach is to use a range from the 1st to 99th percentiles to accommodate a greater-than-usual segment of the population of potential users. However, these wider limits may only confuse two key issues: (1) which percentiles offer the best economic payoff and (2) which means and standard deviations are appropriate for the user populations.

Two major anthropometric problems face furniture designers in the United States today. One is the lack of really good anthropometric data on civilian office workers. No survey in the last three decades has provided sufficient and accurate data on a large number of dimensions of civilians in the United States. Analyses attempting to match the data of Air Force populations to data from a survey of civilians during 1960–1962 (McConville et al., 1981) have been promising but incomplete for purposes of developing a full set of anthropometric criteria for workstation design. Furthermore, such studies have not been updated to adjust for later (but less comprehensive) data on civilians measured in 1971–1974 or in 1976–1980.

The best data on Americans today may be those on the dimensions of men and women of the U.S. Army, measured during 1987–1988 (Gordon et al., 1989b). Of course, these surveys of military personnel do not adequately represent the wide range of heavy and thin people or of many recent immigrants in the civilian population. Many designers are just learning of the availability of the Army data, and few have had an opportunity to study and apply them to actual designs.

Admittedly, a credible set of predicted and estimated dimensions is easier to conceive than to compile. I have devoted many hours to one step of such an analysis: attempting to "design" an anthropometric standard for the population of U.S. engineers and office workers for the decade 1990–2000. In making this forecast, I have used relatively meager historical change data for civilians, mainly Stature and Weight from the three large surveys mentioned earlier. My estimates of other dimensions were largely based on regressions and ratios derived from military population data, but they reflected the wider ranges of Stature and Weight of civilians. I also accounted for expected age ranges and selection factors that correlate with Stature and Weight, such as number of years of education (13 or more) and the percentage of Blacks in the general population (about 10% as compared with about 25% in the Army).

The results of this effort are not yet ready for publication, but they strongly suggest that a combination of demographic analyses and studies of secular trends could be successfully pursued to develop design data that are more comprehensive and appropriate than currently available data.

Another major problem facing designers of all types of equipment is the lack of a coherent and believable procedure for deciding, on the basis of economics, what percentile ranges should be used for design. The use of the 1st and 99th percentiles may, indeed, be a correct business decision that ensures the maximum benefit to users within acceptable costs. However, I feel more comfortable with a range from the 2nd percentile to the 98th for major dimensions (Height, Sitting Height, Buttock-Knee Length) but would seek a wider range for smaller dimensions such as Hand Length, Foot Length, and Thigh Clearance Height. I have seen no published economic analysis that supports either approach or offers another. I can only hope that the problem of economic payoff will be solved in a rational, analytical manner some day. Until then, we must develop design standards by intuition.

Design Standards

It is possible to find many recommendations in recent human factors publications regarding standards for anthropometric data and the methods for their use in the design of computer workstations (also called video display terminals, or VDTs). A landmark example is the standard ANSI/HFS 100-1988, prepared by members of the Human Factors and Ergonomics Society (1988) for the American National Standards Institute (ANSI). Fortunately, the authors of this standard recognized that particular designs may have different needs than can be foreseen and recommended in terms of specific numerical dimensions. They therefore provided both general solutions and specific solutions for design problems. The general solutions are relatively independent of the actual range of population dimensions and stress general principles of design. Conversely, specific numerical recommendations are also offered, based on a set of tabulated anthropometric data, representing the authors' best guess as to the dimensions applicable for a wide range of civilian applications. These data are given in Table 5.

TABLE 5
Anthropometric Values for VDT Furniture Design Standards per
ANSI/HFS 100-1988 in cm(in)

	5th percentile female/male	95th percentile female/male
Buttock-Knee Length	51.8(20.4)/54.0(21.3)	62.5(24.6)/64.2(25.3)
Buttock-Popliteal Length	40.9(16.1)/45.0(17.1)	47.2(18.6)/50.5(19.9)
Elbow-Fingertip Length	38.5(15.2)/44.1(17.4)	46.0(18.1)/51.4(20.2)
Elbow Rest Height (sitting)	18.1(7.1)/19.0(7.5)	28.1(11.0)/29.4(11.6)
Eye Height (sitting)	67.5(26.6)/72.6(28.6)	78.5(30.9)/84.4(33.2)
Foot Length	22.3(8.8)/24.8(9.8)	26.2(10.3)/29.0(11.4)
Hip Breadth	31.2(12.3)/30.8(12.1)	43.7(17.2)/40.6(16.0)
Knee Height (sitting)	45.2(17.8)/49.3(19.4)	54.4(21.5)/59.3(23.3)
Popliteal Height	35.5(14.0)/39.2(15.4)	44.3(17.4)/48.8(19.2)
Thigh Height (above seat)	10.6(4.2)/11.4(4.5)	17.5(6.9)/17.7(7.0)

The anthropometric data in this table provide the information needed to determine compliance with Section 8, "Furniture," on page 41 of the ANSI/HFS 100-1988 standard. All the measures except the buttock-popliteal length are U.S. civilian body dimensions for ages 20 to 60 years as determined by J. T. McConville, Anthropology Research Project, Yellow Springs, Ohio, and K. W. Kennedy, USAF-AMRL-HEG, and presented by Kroemer (1985). The buttock-popliteal length is based on military data and was excerpted from McConville and Laubach (1978).

A major revision of ANSI/HFS 100-1988 is under way as of this writing. Figure 48 shows examples of the use of anthropometric data to develop design limits for acceptable postures and dimensions of workstation furniture, especially seat height and keyboard height.

Recommendations for VDT work space design often focus strongly on heights of keyboards, tables, seats, and screens. Height is important, but more consideration should be given to the interactions of height with the

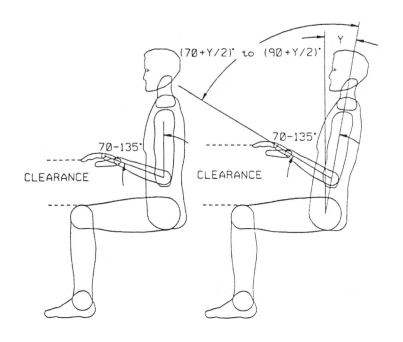

orientations of armrests, keyboards, and seat backs. In other words, the work-space and human together should be treated as a system, rather than a set of isolated rules for design.

Note in Figure 48 (above and right) some relatively general postural limits for design. These provide criteria for specific height dimensions (in centimeters and inches) for seats and keyboards that are included lower on the figure, based on the assumed set of dimensions of VDT operators in Table 5.

Controversies about Postures

A major concern in computer workstation design has centered on correct posture. Voluminous literature offers advice based on the erect posture recommended for typing. It seems that many ergonomics specialists have failed to recognize the rapid change in flexibility of design offered by modern computers. Keyboard heights, angles, and shapes need not be the same as those on old, mechanically constrained typewriters. Heights and angles of the keyboard (or mouse support plate) now can be — and should be — coordinated with the orientations of other desirable supports, such as backward-leaning chairs, split keyboards, and armrests, to achieve comfortable wrist, elbow, and upper arm angles, regardless of the height of the chair or its supporting surface slopes. Chair height is not a simple variable but depends on the type of work, length of tasks, and presence or absence of footrests.

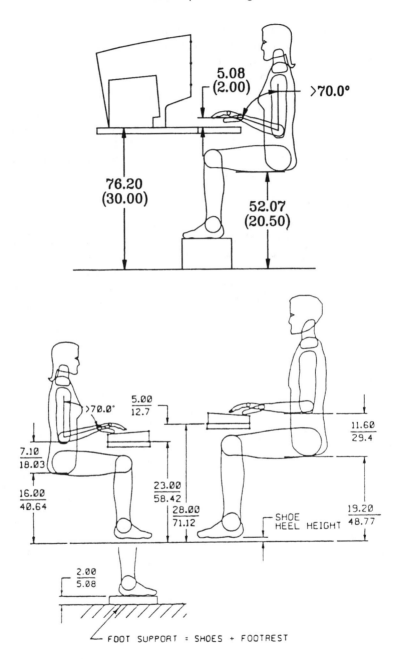

Figure 48. Anthropometric dimensions determining the geometry of computer workstations (Human Factors and Ergonomics Society, 1988).

Observations of VDT operators show that they adopt a remarkably wide range of postures, well outside those typically displayed in recommendations for "correct" posture. And why not? Frequent changes of posture are highly recommended for sedentary work.

Obviously, designing for a range of postural options carries with it a cost in adjustability and must be considered in conjunction with the demands of the job. Again, using principles of systems engineering will help to design a useful range of adjustments and work-rest cycles that eliminate or minimize pain and injury from long hours of repeated activities in a fixed posture, while supporting goals of high productivity and social and economic benefits.

Special Measuring Devices

ANSI/HFS 100-1988 contains recommended practices comparable to those for standardizing methods for particular measurements in aircraft and automotive design. Devices and procedures are described for measurements of upholstered seat height, seat reference point, seat angles, back height, and seat depth. Thus, the general methods described for dynamic vehicle environments also apply to this relatively static and common workplace situation.

Chapter 8

DESIGN AND EVALUATION OF TOOLS, CONTROLS, COMPONENTS, AND EQUIPMENT

Hand Tools and Handles

The design of tools that are grasped or operated by humans has much in common with the design of handles and other handheld devices. The principal anthropometric considerations are the shape, size, and capabilities of the fingers, thumb, palm, and wrist. Other major concerns (mostly omitted in this chapter) involve finger mobility and strength. Fortunately, several researchers have made anthropometric measurements of the hands of large numbers of military personnel, both male and female. Useful introductory documents include Garrett (1970, 1971), Vicinus (1962), and Czaja (1984), as well as those in Table 3 (see page 83).

Computer modeling of hands has highlighted the need for detailed anthropometry of hands, including definitions of links and external dimensions of length, breadth, and depth of each segment. A thesis by Buchholz (1989) included references to much of the literature on modeling and presents his breakthrough measurements of functional, interjoint link lengths for six cadavers. Still, the human factors literature relating dimensions to design applications is sparse, and the connections between anthropometry and functional requirements are often not well defined (for example, see Armstrong, 1985).

Typical handbook data on hand access clearance requirements often fail even to suggest any relationships to hand size, except for the type of glove worn. Despite the thousands of years that people have been making and using tools, the hand-tool interface remains ripe for more definitive research.

Controls

Controls typically are divided into manual and pedal types, and the anthropometric concerns are quite different between the two. Like tools, controls are handled by humans but usually are more or less permanently attached to components, consoles, or vehicles. Many power tools are operated by controls such as triggers, slide switches, buttons, thumb nuts, and knobs.

Finger diameters, lengths, contours, and comfort angles are common types of data needed for applications.

A control design problem that arises frequently is the maximum torque that can be exerted on control knobs, tools, and connectors. Although torque measurements are not treated in this book, the relation of hand size to effectiveness of grasp is. Data of this kind are especially relevant when a control is to be recessed below the surface of a panel to reduce chances of inadvertent operation.

I measured the hands of 14 subjects as part of a control knob torque strength study (Roebuck, 1965) and found that subjective judgments of comfort and effectiveness of control for recessed bar knobs were related to certain measurements of the lengths of finger segments. Figure 49 shows some of these key relationships.

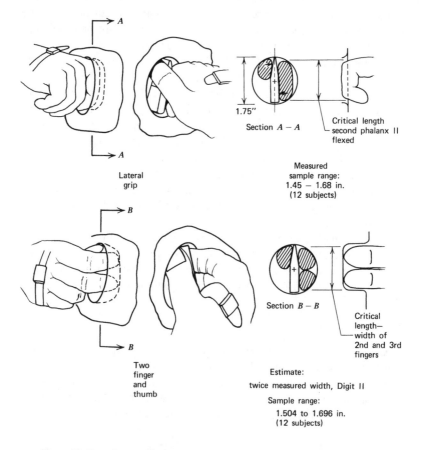

Figure 49. Control recess diameter is related to finger dimensions (Roebuck, 1965).

Components

Components are items such as electronic black boxes and their contents, pumps, motors, valves, and other items of complex systems that may be handled during installation or maintenance. Though often not specifically designed to fit a range of hand or foot sizes, they may be fitted with handles, rounded corners, indentations, or gripping areas that are influenced by the needs of people who deal with them. Also of concern for maintenance and assembly are the free spaces around equipment that are needed for finger, hand, and glove access during installation and removal.

For example, consider the design of a computer-based trainer (Figure 50) that is operated by thumb switches arranged in an arc, with instructional material displayed on a small liquid-crystal screen (Gilbert, Hahn, Gilmore, and Schurman, 1988). The designers found few useful data on thumb reach anthropometry. Their response was to make some special measurements of the range of thumb motion while holding a mockup box of the expected dimensions for the equipment item (Figure 51). They also had to define some new terminology for their measurements. For example, *thumb reach* was defined as the length of the thumb from the crotch to the thumb tip. Although this term was defined by Garrett (1971) as *thumb length*, Gilbert et al. (1988) believed that because they considered thumb rotation as part of the action, they were measuring reach rather than simply length.

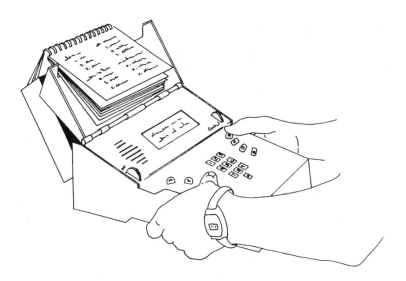

Figure 50. Thumb-controlled, computer-based trainer device (Gilbert et al., 1988).

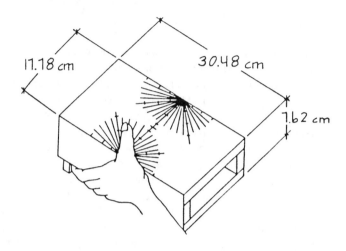

Figure 51. Special device for measuring thumb reach (Gilbert et al., 1988).

Table 6 presents some results of Gilbert et al.'s study. Their analysis also showed that reach measures for the right and left hand were highly correlated and different for the two sexes. However, these measurements were not significantly related to age or handedness.

TABLE 6
Thumb Anthropometry for Males (First Line) and Females (Second Line)

Dimension	Mean	Standard Deviation	5th Percentile	95th Percentile
Thumb reach at	6.95	0.67	5.77	8.03
0 deg	6.28	0.82	5.13	7.69
Thumb reach at	6.90	0.67	5.77	8.03
45 deg	6.23	0.69	5.31	7.38
Thumb reach at	6.77	0.69	5.77	7.69
90 deg	6.15	0.54	5.31	6.90
Most comfortable	55	14.97	33	86
angular displacement	54	13.59	34	85
Maximum angular	115	10.33	100	132
displacement	115	8.77	107	133
Thumb reach at maximum	6.80	0.74	5.46	7.69
angular displacement	5.90	0.59	4.97	6.90

Source: Gilbert, Hahn, Gilmore, and Schurman (1988)
Note: Measurements are in centimeters or degrees, as appropriate.

Personal Equipment

Personal equipment includes a large assortment of items including some of the foregoing, depending on one's method of classification. These items constitute a gray area between clothing (discussed in Chapter 9) and components. They are typically attached to or carried by humans and often consist of rigid units that are attached to the body or stabilized by flexible straps or similar methods. Examples include a diver's scuba gear, backpacks for hikers and firefighters, astronauts' space suits, flotation devices, miners' lights, lanterns, and tool or weapon holsters. Many prosthetic devices can also be considered in this category.

For sizing and location of straps or belts, anthropometric data usually can aid in the determination of circumferential adjustment requirements, lengths for distances between key joints or landmarks, and contours of pads. Anthropometric measurement techniques and equipment (such as used for casting or contour measurement procedures) may be required for custom-fitted parts, especially prostheses.

Chapter 9

CLOTHING DESIGN AND FIT TESTING

General Clothing Design Process

The generalized, step-by-step process for the design of clothing in Figure 52 is heavily influenced by procedures in the development of military clothing. As with equipment design, military clothing design must include selection of the design population and associated compilations of anthropometric data. Because of major investments in anthropometric surveys, the U.S. armed forces have available massive amounts of statistical data specifically gathered to aid clothing design and definition of distribution strategies.

Extensive data are lacking for the civilian sector of the United States, though other nations, such as Japan, Korea, England, and Germany, have conducted large-scale surveys for clothing standardization. Consequently, the design of clothing for U.S. civilians is probably based more on market forces that determine what sells and on the hard-won experience of tailors who have learned their trade through apprenticeships. Because information of this kind is commercial and often proprietary in nature, little has been written or published on how the process is carried out. However, some parts of the civilian sector have begun to use computer analysis for pattern development and some forms of data gathering.

Sizing for Fit and Tariffs

Major aspects of anthropometric applications to clothing design are deciding how to size various types of clothing and how many of what size to buy for intended populations (clothing tariffs). Tebbetts, McConville, and Alexander (1979) described this work as divided into six steps that mainly encompass work in Blocks 2 and 3 of Figure 52. The following description conforms to the authors' step numbers, with numbering from Figure 52 in parentheses.

Step 1 (Block 2)
First, select an appropriate body of data for analysis, as described in Chapter 7 for work space design.

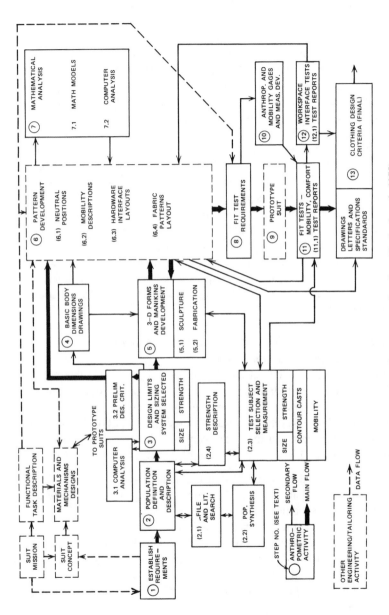

Figure 52. Clothing design process flowchart (Roebuck et al., 1975).

149

Step 2 (Block 3) Select the Key or Sizing Dimensions

Select the key dimensions on which the design ranges of other dimensions will be based. Extensive statistical studies of correlations between dimensions show that height and weight provide the two most effective dimensions for many items of military clothing (Emanuel, Alexander, Churchill, and Truett, 1959), especially those that must be closely fitted over a large portion of the body surface. However, as everyone knows, men's dress shirts in Europe, North America, and most cosmopolitan business communities are sized by neck circumference and sleeve length. This sizing method is responsive to the current Western style of dress that calls for a close-fitting collar and sleeves that reach to the wrists. These dimensions are actual design criteria — dimensions for the finished product — but a good overall fit still depends on different cuts or styles (e.g., tapered or full).

The design of men's shirts must allow for considerable looseness of fit around the chest and waist, except for people who are very heavy in relation to their height. Note that even in this case, one dimension is related to body mass (neck circumference) and the other to body linear dimensions (sleeve length).

For women's blouses, sizes are frequently related to bust circumference and sleeve length; the prevailing styles generally do not call for a close fit around the neck.

Step 3 (Block 3) Select Intervals for the Key Dimensions that Will Establish Each Size Category

Divide the combinations of these dimensions into suitable intervals or categories and a definition of the design ranges (specific dimensions for fitting fabric) for each size. Exactly how this process is accomplished is not well explained in the literature, probably because it depends on the judgment of experienced people and involves many complex trade-offs among the following factors:

- number of sizes already specified by previous needs;
- maximum permissible width of a sizing category in terms of the key dimensions (if specified);
- possible range of adjustability within the end item;
- material the garment will be made of (elastic or nonelastic);
- the closeness of fit desired (snug for a partial pressure suit, loose for fatigues or informal dress); and
- whether the garment is a single-piece coverall or a combination of blouse and trousers.

Ideally, sizes should be few in number and distributed relatively evenly through the population so that economies of mass production can be realized in making patterns and cutting cloth. Other desirable objectives are to minimize the amount of cloth needed and to provide a comfortable and effective fit of the garment to each customer. Precise procedures and weighting factors to accommodate these objectives are difficult to put into writing. To some degree, the process seems to depend on cut-and-try approaches.

Step 4 (Block 3) Develop the Dimensional Data for Each of the Established Size Categories

Once a proposed number of sizes and their associated intervals for the key dimensions are defined, subsequent statistical analysis procedures are clearly definable, and the results of trying each option can be well quantified (Anthropology Research Project staff, 1978a; Emanuel et al., 1959). Studies of military clothing requirements provide useful information about how to optimize designs in light of conflicting requirements. For example, these analyses have shown that for many garment designs based on height and weight, only six to nine sizes are reasonable, and the design range for specific circumferences and lengths should cover 1.5 to 2 times the standard deviation of the data for people within each size interval. With the possibility of upgrading to the next size, such a process can accommodate up to 95% of a population such as can be found in the military services.

Figure 53 illustrates one way of dividing up the bivariate distribution data on Height and Weight to define size intervals for eight sizes of men's clothing for flying personnel in the U.S. Air Force. Other studies have defined 6-, 9-, and 12-size divisions for different purposes (Emanuel et al., 1959).

Step 5 (Block 3) Convert the Summary Data into the Appropriate Design Values

Sort data on individuals into the size intervals selected for the key dimensions and compute means and standard deviations for each group. In general, these distributions will not be normal or similar from group to group, so the means will not fall exactly in the center of the intervals.

Step 6 (Block 3) Establish the Tariff, or Numbers of Each Size Necessary to Outfit the User Population

Count the number of people who fall into each size interval and express the count as a percentage of the total group. Judgments of how many may be accommodated by upgrading into a different size may affect the final tariff decisions.

Fit Test

In addition to the six steps listed, there is an important seventh step that is frequently ignored in the rush to start manufacture of the garments. This step involves fit testing — accompanied by anthropometric measurements of

HEIGHT (INCHES)

WEIGHT (POUNDS)	61.4–62.2	62.2–63.0	63.0–63.8	63.8–64.5	64.5–65.3	65.3–66.1	66.1–66.9	66.9–67.7	67.7–68.4	68.4–69.3	69.3–70.1	70.1–70.8	70.8–71.6	71.6–72.4	72.4–73.2	73.2–74.0	74.0–74.8	74.8–75.6	75.6–76.4	76.4–77.1	TOTALS
227–232									1	1			1	2	1	2	1	1			10
221–226									2		2		1	2	3	1	1	1	1		14
215–220									3	2	4	2	2	6	1	2	2	1	1		26
209–214						1				2	10	3	9	6	5	5	3	2	3		49
203–208						1		3	5	4	8	10	7	9	8	5	1	4		1	66
197–203				1			1	3	7	12	14	7	23	10	10	7	6	2		2	117
191–196						2	3	9	8	22	23	19	23	17	15	8	1	4	3		160
185–190					1		6	9	18	38	21	22	20	26	7	6	7	1	2	1	200
179–184				1	1	2	11	14	29	36	35	37	22	29	15	6	6	1	1	1	250
173–178				1	3	4	16	26	38	44	54	40	38	26	16	21	7	2	1		345
167–172	1		2	2	5	14	16	30	45	51	61	48	43	26	13	11	7	2	1		386
161–166			3	4	10	20	25	41	51	85	64	56	42	26	16	12	3		1		456
155–160		2	3	5	10	20	32	45	63	76	71	53	48	25	14	9	3	1	2		479
149–154	2		4	8	17	33	36	54	57	52	61	50	39	14	8	3		1	1		443
143–148			2	6	25	28	43	45	51	53	42	53	13	8	7		2		1		363
137–142	2	3	6	13	14	33	49	46	43	32	32	34	12	6	3	2					319
131–136	2	1	1	9	12	24	27	27	30	13	14	23	3								117
125–130	2	4	3	10	11	22	12	13	16	10		11	1								110
119–124		1	3	5	8	8	4	7	5												42
113–118		1	1	3	2	2	1	2	1												13
TOTALS	9	15	28	68	119	214	282	374	473	533	515	468	347	241	143	100	50	23	18	5	4025

r = 0.47

Figure 53. Partitioning a Height-Weight scatter diagram into several clothing sizes (Emanuel et al., 1959).

152

the subjects — of prototype garments to determine if the sizing scheme that was developed is correct for the type of garment being produced. Emanuel et al. (1959) described this process; additional descriptions and examples of results have also appeared in a variety of reports issued by the Aerospace Medical Research Laboratory (e.g., Alexander, McConville, Kramer, and Fritz, 1964; McConville, Tebbetts, and Alexander, 1979).

Strength Data

You may wonder how human strength data enter into the design of clothing. These concerns may arise in the design of pressure suits and life support packs associated with protective clothing. The design of suit mobility joints may create significant resistance to joint motion, such that muscular strength becomes a factor in survival. As more complex life support gear is added, the total suit system may become extremely heavy, possibly more than the weight of the user. Even on the moon or in space, the mass of protective clothing may impede work. Also, people wearing pressure suits have to use considerable force to compensate for the rigidity produced by the pressure differential between the interior and exterior of the suit. Finally, pressure suits usually require wearers to operate knobs and switches to control the various communication, stowage, and environmental control functions.

Body Forms

Tailors and homemakers have long recognized the difficulty of designing accurate flat patterns on flexible material so that clothing will fit comfortably and stylishly on the complex, three-dimensional curves of the human body. An approach used for many years has been to develop patterns on 3D forms that have been designed and constructed to resemble different sizes and shapes of human bodies. In many cases, these forms were made of adjustable materials that could be manipulated to approximate an individual's circumferences and other key contour measurements. For a complete line of ready-made clothing sizes, many standardized forms would be required. Therefore, careful attention has been given to developing statistically valid forms for large populations, such as military pilots, for whom good fit is often as much a matter of survival as a "soldierly appearance" (McConville, Alexander, and Velsey, 1963; Zeigen, Alexander, Churchill, Emanuel, and Velsey, 1960).

In practice, traditional anthropometric survey data are not complete enough for the design of accurate forms. Although many circumferences are usually measured, to develop 3D forms requires accurate data on linear offsets of key body protrusions and valleys (especially in anterior-posterior directions) from some common axes. Offset data of this kind were partially supplied by one (relatively rare) study that sought to develop 3D hard plaster dummies representing contours of the body that are typical of several sizes of military personnel (McConville et al., 1963).

Figure 54 illustrates the type of depth offset data that were obtained from photographic records of a group of young Air Force pilots. A trained sculptor then transformed the standard anthropometric measures and offsets into approximately correct plaster shapes for the forms, built up on armatures of metal angles and wire.

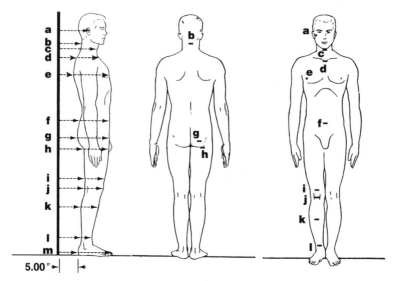

Figure 54. Depth offsets for 3D dummy development
(McConville et al., 1963).

Physical forms for feet, hands, and heads are generally developed separately from the torso, but in their development, you may encounter many of the same statistical concerns. For feet, the form is called a *last*. More than a sculpture of the foot, it is designed to act as the mold shape for the interior of shoes and boots. Therefore, lasts include some space for toes to extend and perhaps wiggle a little (at least for some men's shoes) and are, to a significant degree, determined by the shape of the shoe.

Contours

Although sculptural methods based on carefully selected anthropometric data are effective, more objective and reproducible methods for measuring, recording, and reproducing complete body contours are now available. Among them are various photographic methods using narrow beams of light, stereophotogrammetry, moiré light photographs, and various laser applications (described in Chapter 3). The most promising seem to be stereo photo contour maps and laser measurements of contours.

However measured and analyzed, one way to present the data for clothing design is with contour maps of the body. From such maps it is theoretically possible to measure the circumferences, surface distances, and point-to-point diameters of segments of the body surfaces. If the contour lines accurately depict the surface shapes at the planes where they were determined, the results developed from these maps should be comparable to those obtained by tape measure directly on the living body, except for the effects of pressures that locally distort surfaces on the skin. Slight errors also may result if the contours measured are widely separated where the body shape changes abruptly.

Another small source of error is that the sum of straight-line chords connecting points on the contour lines or spaces between contour planes may be slightly shorter than the actual curved surfaces on which the tape would lie in a real subject. Therefore, contour maps for clothing design (or for computer modeling of work spaces) should be used cautiously. If you plan to use this kind of data, validate the information by measuring real people using normal tailoring measurements (or anthropometers and calipers for diameters and lengths).

In the design of close-fitting clothing for personnel protection, you should pay careful attention to changes of circumferences and shapes as the arms, legs, and body are flexed and extended, as well as for the static standing posture. However, body forms described in published reports to date have not dealt with these changes. They are most likely considered as a part of the tailoring process, which still depends greatly on experience. For example, the only body form described in the study by McConville et al. (1963) was for a standing posture. The report does include data on many depths and breadths for a sitting posture, from which some allowances might be derived. Most other sources of stereo or laser contour data involve only the standing or prone posture, a problem that must be overcome in the future of imaging technology, not only for clothing design but for other work space design and medical concerns as well.

For smaller parts of the body, such as hands, feet, and heads, casting processes are feasible and have been used for developing individually sized and contoured shapes or to develop standard sizes. Castings can become the basis for tools that are dipped into a fluid, such as liquid rubber or plastic, as a production process for making gloves. Gloves for the early astronaut space suits were developed by this kind of process, and similar methods are used for producing surgical gloves today.

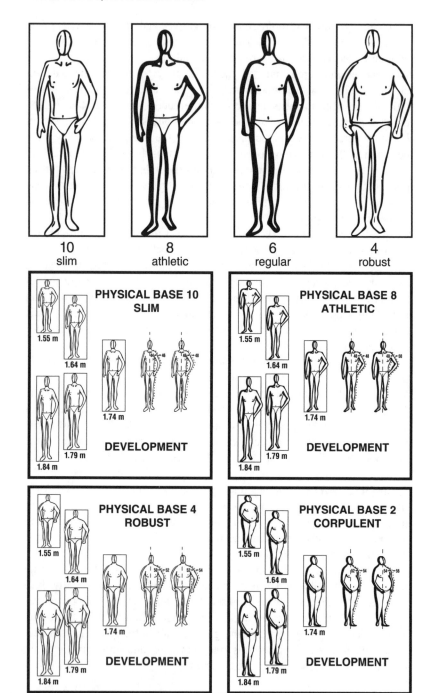

10
slim

8
athletic

6
regular

4
robust

PHYSICAL BASE 10
SLIM

1.55 m

1.64 m

1.74 m

1.79 m

1.84 m

DEVELOPMENT

PHYSICAL BASE 8
ATHLETIC

1.55 m

1.64 m

1.74 m

1.79 m

1.84 m

DEVELOPMENT

PHYSICAL BASE 4
ROBUST

1.55 m

1.64 m

1.74 m

1.79 m

1.84 m

DEVELOPMENT

PHYSICAL BASE 2
CORPULENT

1.55 m

1.64 m

1.74 m

1.79 m

1.84 m

DEVELOPMENT

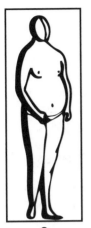

2
corpulent

0
extra corpulent

CONFORMATION 10
Tg. 44-46-48

CONFORMATION 8
Tg. 46-48-50-52-54-56

CONFORMATION 6
Tg. 48-50-52

CONFORMATION 4
Tg. 50-52-54

CONFORMATION 2
Tg. 52-54-56

CONFORMATION 0
Tg. 54-56-58

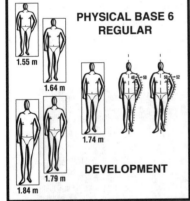

**PHYSICAL BASE 6
REGULAR**

DEVELOPMENT

*Figure 55. Size concepts for male
clothing based on the CAD Modelling
System (courtesy of CAD Modelling).
See text, p. 158.*

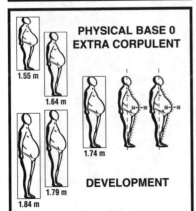

**PHYSICAL BASE 0
EXTRA CORPULENT**

DEVELOPMENT

1,55 m – extra short
1,64 m – short
1,74 m – medium
1,79 m – tall
1,84 m – extra tall

Some types of clothing, such as helmets, have only a small number of basic outer shell contours, and the variations of body size are accommodated by different interior pads or adjustable straps and sling devices. For these designs, anthropometric data can provide information on the range of circumferences required for the adjustments or on the different thicknesses for pads. Because of the wide variety in size and shapes of human heads, great care should be taken in selecting the data and applying them to the design of helmets, face masks, goggles, and other head-mounted gear or optics.

A Computer-Based Civilian Clothing Size Process

CAD Modelling, Inc. of Florence, Italy, developed a proprietary system and equipment for the photographic recording of body silhouettes and for applying computer analysis techniques to develop flat clothing patterns from body outlines (CAD Modelling, 1992). The sizing system is based on a graded series of different body proportions, from wiry to obese. Figure 55 shows the concepts for clothing sizes for males. The company developed 3D forms for each size. As shown in Figure 56, these forms have some joint articulation capabilities that permit the evaluation of the effects of body limb posture on the finished product.

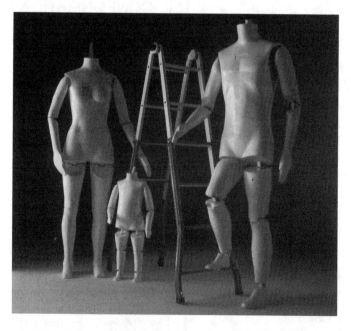

Figure 56. CAD Modelling manikins (courtesy of CAD Modelling).

In practice, the customer enters a booth where a side view and a front-view photograph are taken. The resulting outline contours are then matched as closely as possible to one of the standard silhouettes listed in Figure 55. A computer analysis of differences then estimates the necessary deviations from the standard flat clothing patterns to fit the individual (Figure 57). The suit or other clothing is then custom tailored to the individual.

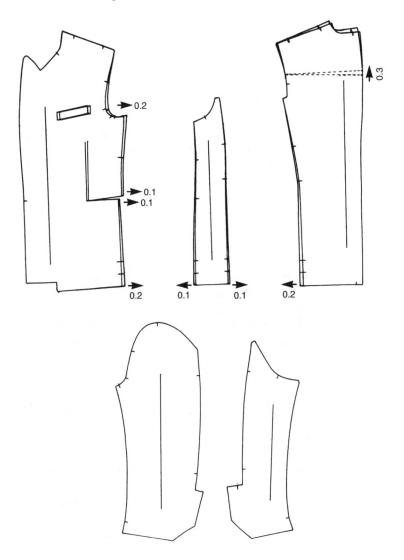

Figure 57. Modification of clothing pattern (courtesy of CAD Modelling).

Chapter 10

SUMMARY AND CONCLUSIONS

In this book, I have surveyed and described a number of anthropometric measurement and application methods. My goals have been to

1. indicate the many options currently available for obtaining useful measurement data;
2. show that even if all desired data have not been directly measured, you can still estimate many useful dimensions (and must do so for forecasts); and
3. explain how anthropometric data can be applied to human factors problems in the development of design criteria and the evaluation of design concepts at various stages of a project, or even as selection and screening methods for workers.

Even if they never measure people, applications personnel must understand measurement methods to use anthropometric data correctly. However, many of them will be required to make some measurements because there are almost never enough of the right data for new applications. I have also identified several areas where future research can significantly improve the level of understanding and accuracy of data, as well as the efficiency of measurements and applications. Forecasting anthropometric dimensions was recommended for all applications, especially for long-term development projects.

A major theme running throughout this book is that trends toward the use of computers for modeling humans demand a major shift in future measurement goals. It is no longer sufficient to define single-valued diameters, lengths, and circumferences. Dimensions need to be defined in terms of 3D coordinates. Also, the dimensions and postures selected should permit you to determine locations of effective joint centers of rotation and help you to define body surface contours. Furthermore, measurement procedures and dimensional data reporting should be geared toward descriptions of body segment proportions and relative variability comparisons between different segments as well as simple means, standard deviations, and correlations.

Another major point is that new electronic imaging technology has an increasing impact on anthropometric methods, providing more accurate and full definition of human form but creating a new challenge concerning how to analyze and summarize the massive new data sets.

I have also shown that there is a trend away from the use of common-percentile manikins for design criteria in favor of determination of true percentage accommodation. The latter goal is what the concept of percentiles was supposed to accomplish, but it is accurate for only one dimension at a time. Current design requirements for many applications — including work spaces, equipment, and clothing — frequently involve limitations related to several key dimensions simultaneously. Some industries rely on multiple-subject mockup testing alone to develop these percentage accommodation statistics, whereas others are developing Monte Carlo and principal component analysis methods suitable for computer-generated human models. Fortunately, the increased power of computer workstations has permitted more sophisticated statistical analysis than in the past and made it possible to complete such analyses in a timely manner.

In addition to introducing the field of anthropometry to potential new ergonomists, I have also pointed out interactions of anthropometric content and methods with the content and methods used by specialists with other human factors and life science experts.

Finally, I have included some general lessons learned from industrial experience. These include a general philosophy distilled from years of daily interaction with engineers and the real-world problems of development projects. Although cast in the context of anthropometry, these comments could apply to many human factors activities.

REFERENCES

Abraham, S., Johnson, C. L., and Najjar, M. F. (1979). *Weight and height of adults 18–74 years of age, United States, 1971–1974* (data from National Health Survey, Series 11, No. 211). Hyattsville, MD: National Center for Health Statistics.

Ad Hoc Working Group on Design Guidelines. (1991). *Model guidelines for accessible lavatories in twin aisle aircraft* (Final draft, ATA Document 91-XX). Washington, DC: Air Transport Association of America.

Alexander, M., McConville, J. T., Kramer, J. H., and Fritz, E. A. (1964). *Height-weight sizing of protective garments, based on Japanese air self-defense force pilot data, with fit-test results* (AMRL-TDR-64-66). Wright-Patterson Air Force Base, OH: Behavioral Sciences Laboratory, Aerospace Medical Research Laboratory.

Annis, J. F., Case, H. W., Clauser, C. E., and Bradtmiller, B. (1991). Anthropometry of an aging work force. *Experimental Aging Research, 17*(3), 157–176.

Annis, J. F., and McConville, J. T. (1990). Applications of anthropometric data in sizing and design. In B. Das (Ed.), *Advances in industrial ergonomics and safety II.* London: Taylor & Francis.

Anthropology Research Project staff. (Eds.). (1978a). *Anthropometric source book. Volume I: Anthropometry for designers* (NASA Reference Publication 1024). Houston: NASA Scientific and Technical Information Office.

Anthropology Research Project staff. (Eds.). (1978b). *Anthropometric source book. Volume II: A handbook of anthropometric data* (NASA Reference Publication 1024). Houston: NASA Scientific and Technical Information Office.

Anthropology Research Project staff. (Eds.). (1978c). *Anthropometric source book. Volume III: Annotated bibliography of anthropometry* (NASA Reference Publication 1024). Houston: NASA Scientific and Technical Information Office.

Architectural and Transportation Barriers Compliance Board. (1982, August 4). Minimum guidelines and requirements for accessible design. 36 CFR Part 1190 *Federal Register, 47*(150). Includes many reach and clearance requirements for persons with disabilities who require wheelchairs, as well as other architectural features and space requirements for ambulatory persons.

Armstrong, T. J. (1985). *Biomechanical aspects of the upper extremity in work.* Ann Arbor: Department of Environmental and Industrial Health, University of Michigan.

Badler, N. I., Phillips, C. B., and Webber, B. L. (1993). *Simulating humans, computer graphic animation and control.* New York: Oxford University Press.

Berol Corporation. (1976). *R-1052 Human figure, 50th percentile male 1/4 scale.* Berol RapiDesign, Berol USA, Division of Berol Corporation, 345 Parkside Dr., P.O. Box 990, San Fernando, CA 91340.

Bittner, A. C. (1975). *Computerized accommodated percentage evaluation (CAPE) model for cockpit analysis and exclusion studies* (Tech. Publication TP-75-49/TIP-03). Point Mugu, CA: Pacific Missile Test Center.

Bittner, A. C., Dannhaus, D. M., and Roth, J. T. (1975). Workplace-accommodated percentage evaluation: Model and preliminary results. In M. M. Ayoub and C. G. Halcomb (Eds.), *Improved seat, console and workplace design.* Point Mugu, CA: Pacific Missile Test Center.

Boughner, R. L. (1991). *A model of average adult male human skeletal and leg muscle geometry and hamstring length for automotive seating designers.* Unpublished master's thesis, Michigan State University, East Lansing, MI.

Boyle, E., Ianni, J., Easterly, J., Harper, S., and Korna, M. (1991). *Human-centered technology for maintainability: Workshop proceedings* (AL-TP-1991-0010). Wright-Patterson Air Force Base, OH: Armstrong Laboratory, Human Resources Directorate, Logistics Research Division.

Breaking New Ground Resource Center. (1986). *Agricultural tools, equipment, machinery & buildings for farmers and ranchers with physical handicaps.* West Lafayette, IN: Purdue University, Department of Agricultural Engineering.

Buchholz, B. O. (1989). *A kinematic model of the human hand to evaluate its prehensile capabilities.* Doctoral dissertation, University of Michigan, Ann Arbor, MI.

Burdi, A., Huelke, D. F., Snyder, R. G., and Lowrey, G. H. (1969). Infants and children in the adult world of automotive safety design: Pediatric and anatomical considerations for the design of vehicle restraints. *Journal of Biomechanics, 2,* 267–280.

Burke, P. H., and Beard, L. F. H. (1967). Stereophotogrammetry of the face. *American Journal of Orthodontics, 53,* 769–782.

CAD Modelling. (1992). Sales brochure. Piazza Beccaria n.6 50121 Florence, Italy: Author.

Carlyle, L. (1960). *Man and space* (Engineering Paper 899). El Segundo, CA: Douglas Aircraft Co.

Chaffee, J. W. (1961). *The effect of acceleration on human centers of gravity* (Unpublished report FZY-013). Fort Worth, TX: General Dynamics Corp., Convair Division.

Chaffee, J. W. (1969). *Methods for determining driver reach capability* (SAE Report 690105) New York: Society of Automotive Engineers.

Chandler, R. F., Clauser, C. E., McConville, J. T., Reynolds, H. M., and Young, J. W. (1975). *Investigation of the inertial properties of the human body* (DOT-HS-801 430, AMRL-TR-74-137). Washington, DC: U.S. Department of Transportation, National Highway Traffic Safety Administration.

Chapanis, A. (Ed.). (1975). *Ethnic variables in human factors engineering.* Baltimore: Johns Hopkins University Press.

Cheverud, J., Gordon, C. C., Walker, R. A., Jacquish, C., Kohn, L., Moore, A., and Yamashita, N. (1990a). *1988 Anthropometric survey of U.S. Army personnel: Correlation coefficients and regression equations, Part 2. Simple and partial correlation tables — male* (Tech. Report Natick/TR-90/033). Natick, MA: U.S. Army Natick Research, Development and Engineering Center.

Cheverud, J., Gordon, C. C., Walker, R. A., Jacquish, C., Kohn, L., Moore, A., and Yamashita, N. (1990b). *1988 Anthropometric survey of U.S. Army personnel: Correlation coefficients and regression equations, Part 3. Simple and partial correlation tables — female* (Tech. Report Natick/TR-90/034). Natick, MA: U.S. Army Natick Research, Development and Engineering Center.

Cheverud, J., Gordon, C. C., Walker, R. A., Jacquish, C., Kohn, L., Moore, A., and Yamashita, N. (1990c). *1988 Anthropometric survey of U.S. Army personnel: Correlation coefficients and regression equations, Part 4. Bivariate regression tables* (Tech. Report Natick/TR-90/035). Natick, MA: U.S. Army Natick Research, Development and Engineering Center.

Cheverud, J., Gordon, C. C., Walker, R. A., Jacquish, C., Kohn, L., Moore, A., and Yamashita, N. (1990d). *1988 Anthropometric survey of U.S. Army personnel: Correlation coefficients and regression equations, Part 5. Stepwise and standard multiple regression tables* (Tech. Report Natick/TR-90/036). Natick, MA: U.S. Army Natick Research, Development and Engineering Center.

Churchill, E. (1978). Statistical considerations in man-machine designs. In Anthropology Research Project staff (Eds.), *Anthropometric source book, Vol. 1: Anthropometry for designers* (NASA Reference Publication 1024). Houston: NASA Scientific and Technical Information Office.

Churchill, E., Kitka, P., and Churchill, T. (1977). *Intercorrelations of anthropometric measurements: A source book for USA data* (AMRL-TR-77-1). Wright-Patterson Air Force Base, OH: Aerospace Medical Research Laboratory.

Churchill, E., and McConville, J. T. (1976). *Sampling and data gathering strategies for future USAF anthropometry* (AMRL-TR-74-102). Wright-Patterson Air Force Base, OH: Aerospace Medical Research Laboratory, Aerospace Medical Division, (AFSC).

Churchill, T. D., Bradtmiller, B., and Gordon, C. C. (1988). *Computer software used in U.S. Army anthropometric survey 1987-1988* (Tech. Report NATICK/TR-88/045). Natick, MA: U.S. Army Natick Research, Development and Engineering Center.

Clauser, C., McConville, J., and Young, J. W. (1969). *Weight, volume and center of mass of segments of the human body* (AMRL-TR-69-70 [AD 710 622]). Wright-Patterson Air Force Base, OH: Aerospace Medical Research Laboratory.

Clauser, C., Tebbetts, I., Bradtmiller, B., Ervin, C., Annis, J., McConville, J., and Gordon, C. (1987). *Measurer's handbook: U.S. Army anthropometric survey, 1987–1988* (draft, U.S. Army contract DAAK60-86-C-0128). Yellow Springs, OH: Anthropology Research Project, Inc.

Clauser, C. E., Tucker, P. E., McConville, J. T., Churchill, E., Laubach, L. L., and Reardon, J. A. (1972). *Anthropometry of Air Force women* (AMRL TR-70-5). Wright-Patterson Air Force Base, OH: Aerospace Medical Research Laboratory.

Croney, J. (1971). *Anthropometrics for designers.* London: B.T. Batsford/New York: Van Nostrand Reinhold.

CSERIAC (Crew Systems Ergonomics Information Analysis Center). (1991). Working group on electronic imaging of whole body. *CSERIAC Gateway, 2*(4), 8.

Culver, C. C., and Viano, D. C. (1990). Anthropometry of seated women during pregnancy: Defining a fetal region for crash protection research. *Human Factors, 32,* 625–636.

Cyberware. (1990). Sales information for Rapid 3D color digitizer model 3030. Monterey, CA: Author.

Czaja, S. (1984). *Hand anthropometrics. Technical paper with comments.* Washington, DC: U.S. Architectural and Transportation Barriers Compliance Board.

Damon, A., and McFarland, R. A. (1955). The physique of bus and truck drivers: With a review of occupational anthropology. *American Journal of Physiological Anthropology, 2,* 293–316.

Damon, A., and Stoudt, H. W. (1963). The functional anthropometry of old men. *Human Factors, 2,* 485–491.

Damon, A., Stoudt, H. W., and McFarland, R. A. (1966). *The human body in equipment design.* Cambridge, MA: Harvard University Press.

Daniels, G. S. (1952). *The "average man"?* (Tech. Note WCRD 53-7). Wright-Patterson Air Force Base, OH: Wright Air Development Center.

Dempster, W. T. (1955). *Space requirements of the seated operator. Geometrical, kinematic and mechanical aspects of the body with special reference to the limbs* (WADC TR 33-159). Wright-Patterson Air Force Base, OH: Wright Air Development Center.

Devlin, W. A., and Roe, R. (1968). *The eyellipse and considerations in the driver's forward field of view* (SAE Paper 680105). Warrendale, PA: Society of Automotive Engineers.

Diffrient, N., Tilley, A., and Bardagjy, J. C. (1974). *Humanscale 1/2/3.* Cambridge, MA: MIT Press.

Diffrient, N., Tilley, A., and Harman, D. (1981). *Humanscale 4/5/6/7/8/9.* Cambridge, MA: MIT Press.

Dixon, W. J., and Massey, F. J. (1951). *Introduction to statistical analysis.* New York: McGraw-Hill.

Donelson, S. M., and Gordon, C. C. (1991). *1988 Anthropometric survey of U.S. Army personnel: Pilot summary statistics* (Report NATICK/TR-90/040). Natick, MA: U.S. Army Natick Research, Development and Engineering Center.

Dreyfuss, H. (1971). *The measure of man: Human factors in design* (2nd ed.). New York: Whitney Library of Design.

Emanuel, I., Alexander, M., Churchill, E., and Truett, B. (1959). *A height-weight sizing system for flight clothing* (WADC Tech. Report 56-356). Wright-Patterson Air Force Base, OH: Wright Air Development Center, Air Research and Development Command.

Fleck, J. T., Butler, F. E., and Vogel, S. L. (1975). *An improved three dimensional computer simulation of vehicle crash victims. Volume III: User manual* (Report ZQ-5180-L-1). Buffalo, NY: Calspan Corp. Prepared for National Highway Traffic Safety Administration, Department of Transportation.

Garrett, J. W. (1970). *Anthropometry of the Air Force female hand* (AMRL-TR-69-26). Wright-Patterson Air Force Base, OH: Aerospace Medical Research Laboratory.

Garrett, J. W. (1971). The adult human hand: Some anthropometric and biomechanical considerations. *Human Factors, 13,* 236–299.

Garrett, J. W., and Kennedy, K. W. (1971). *A collation of anthropometry* (AAMRL TR-68-1). Wright-Patterson Air Force Base, OH: Aerospace Medical Research Laboratory.

Gavan, J. A. (1950). The consistency of anthropometric measurements. *American Journal of Physiological Anthropology, 8,* 417–426.

Genicom Consultants. (1993). Personal communications and sales presentations. Montreal, Canada: Author.

Gilbert, B. G., Hahn, H. A., Gilmore, W. E., and Schurman, D. L. (1988). Thumbs up: Anthropometry of the first digit. *Human Factors, 30,* 747–750.

Gordon, C. C., and Bradtmiller, B. (1992). Interobserver error in a large scale anthropometric survey. *American Journal of Human Biology, 4,* 253–263.

Gordon, C. C., Churchill, T., Clauser, C. E., Bradtmiller, B., McConville, J. T., Tebbetts, I., and Walker, R. A. (1989a). *1988 Anthropometric survey of U.S. Army personnel: Summary statistics interim report* (Tech. Report Natick/TR-89/027). Natick, MA: U.S. Army Natick Research, Development and Engineering Center.

Gordon, C. C., Churchill, T., Clauser, C. E., Bradtmiller, B., McConville, J. T., Tebbetts, I., and Walker, R. A. (1989b). *1988 Anthropometric survey of U.S. Army personnel: Methods and summary statistics* (Tech. Report Natick/TR-89/044). Natick, MA: U.S. Army Natick Research, Development and Engineering Center.

Gregor, A. (1994, October 12). From PC to factory — computer-aided processes may revolutionize industrial design. *Los Angeles Times,* D1.

Greiner, T. M. (1991). *Hand anthropometry of the U.S. Army personnel* (Report NATICK/TR-92/011). Natick, MA: U.S. Army Natick Research, Development and Engineering Center, Anthropology Branch.

Greiner, T. M., and Gordon, C. C. (1990). *An assessment of long-term changes in anthropometric dimensions: Secular trends of U.S. Army males* (Tech. Report NATICK/TR-91/006). Natick, MA: U.S. Army Natick Research, Development and Engineering Center.

Greiner, T. M., and Gordon, C. C. (1992). Secular trends of 22 body dimensions in four racial/cultural groups of American males. *American Journal of Human Biology, 4,* 235–246.

Gross, C. M. (1991). Mannequin: Human computer-aided design on a PC. *CSERIAC Gateway, 2*(4), 11.

Haas, W. A. (1989). *Geometric model and spinal motions of the average male in seated postures.* Master's thesis, Michigan State University, East Lansing, MI.

Halioua, M., Liu, H. C., Bowins, T. S., and Shih, J. K. (1992). Automated topography of human forms by phase measuring profilometry. In Alberti, Drerup, and Hierholzer (Eds.), *Surface topography and body deformity VI.* Stuttgart and New York: Gustav Fischer Verlag.

Halioua, M., Liu, H. C., Chin, A., and Bowins, T. S. (1990). Automated topography of human forms by phase measuring profilometry and modal analysis. In H. Neugebauer and G. Windischbauer (Eds.), *Surface topography and body deformity V.* Stuttgart and New York: Gustav Fischer Verlag.

Hansen, R., Cornog, D. Y., and Hertzberg, H. T. E. (1958). *Annotated bibliography of applied physical anthropology in human engineering* (WADC Tech. Report 56-30). Wright-Patterson Air Force Base, OH: Aerospace Medical Laboratory.

Harris, R. J. (1975). *A primer of multivariate statistics.* New York: Academic.

Harris, R. J., Bennett, J., and Dow, L. (1980). *CAR-IIA revised model for crewstation assessment of reach* (Tech. Report 1400.06B, Final Report Task 2, Contract N62268-79-C-0235) Willow Grove, PA: Analytics.

Herron, R. E. (1972). *Stereophotogrammetry in biology and medicine* (Unnumbered report). Houston: Texas Institute for Rehabilitation and Research, Baylor College of Medicine, Biostereometrics Laboratory.

Herron, R. E. (1973). Biostereometric measurement of body form. In *Yearbook of physical anthropology 1972* (vol. 16, pp. 80–121). New York: American Association of Physical Anthropologists.

Hertzberg, H. T. E. (1955). Some contributions of applied physical anthropology to human engineering. *Annals of the New York Academy of Science, 63,* 616–629.

Hertzberg, H. T. E. (1968). The conference on standardization of anthropometric techniques and terminology. *American Journal of Physiological Anthropology, 28,* 1–16.

Hertzberg, H. T. E., Churchill, E., Dupertuis, C., White, R., and Damon, A. (1963). *Anthropometric survey of Turkey, Greece and Italy* (AGARDOGraph 73). New York: Macmillan.

Hertzberg, H. T. E., Daniels G. S., and Churchill, E. (1954). *Anthropometry of flying personnel — 1950* (WADC TR 52-321). Wright-Patterson Air Force Base, OH: Wright Air Development Center.

Hooton, E. A. (1945). *A survey in seating.* Gardner, MA: Heywood Wakefield. (Also prepared as undated report: *Survey of measurements relative to dimensions of seats,* Department of Anthropology Statistical Laboratory, Harvard University.)

Human Factors and Ergonomics Society. (1988). *American national standard for human factors engineering of visual display terminal workstations* (ANSI/HFS 100-1988). Santa Monica, CA: Author.

Human Factors Section, Health, Safety and Human Factors Laboratory, Eastman Kodak Company. (1983). *Ergonomic design for people at work. Volume I: Workplace, equipment, and environmental design and information transfer.* London: Lifelong Learning Publications.

Jurgens, H. W., Aune, I. A., and Pieper, U. (1990). *International data on anthropometry* (Occupational Safety and Health Series 65). English edition of the research report *Internationaler anthropometrischer Datenatlas.* Dortmund, Germany: Federal Institute for Occupational Safety and Health. Available from International Labour Organisation, International Labour Office, CH-1211 Geneva 22, Switzerland.

Kelly, P. L., and Kroemer, K. H. E. (1990). Anthropometry of the elderly: Status and recommendations. *Human Factors, 32,* 571–595.

Kennedy, K. W. (1964). *Reach capability of USAF population. Phase 1 — The outer boundaries of grasping — reach envelopes for the shirt-sleeved, seated operator* (AMRL-TDR-64-59). Wright-Patterson Air Force Base, OH: Aerospace Medical Research Laboratory.

Kennedy, K. W. (1986). *A collation of United States Air Force anthropometry (U)* (AAMRL-TR-85-062). Wright-Patterson Air Force Base, OH: Aerospace Medical Research Laboratory, Aerospace Medical Division, Air Force Systems Command.

Kennedy, K. W. (1989). *The UES/Kennedy engineering design manikins — 2-dimensional drawing board design and evaluation aids.* Dayton, OH: Universal Energy Systems, Inc.

Kleeman, W. B. (1987). A different way to use anthropometric data as a tool for computer terminal workstation design. *Human Factors Society Bulletin 30*(2), 4–6.

Kohara, J., and Sugi, T. (1972). *Development of biomechanical manikins for measuring seat comfort* (SAE Paper 720006). New York: Society of Automotive Engineers.

Kroemer, K. H. E. (1985). Office ergonomics: Workstation dimension. In D. C. Alexander and B. M. Pulat (Eds.), *Industrial ergonomics* (pp. 187-201). Norcross, GA: Institute of Industrial Engineers.

Kroemer, K. H. E., Kroemer, H. B., and Kroemer-Elbert, K. E. (1994). *Ergonomics.* Englewood Cliffs, NJ: Prentice-Hall.

Kroemer, K. H. E., Kroemer, H. J., and Kroemer-Elbert, K. E. (1986). *Engineering physiology.* New York: Van Nostrand Reinhold.

Kroemer, K. H. E., Snook, S. H., Meadows, S. K., and Deutsch, S. (Eds.). (1988). *Ergonomic models of anthropometry, human biomechanics, and operator-equipment interfaces. Proceedings of a workshop.* Washington, DC: National Academy Press.

Kyropoulos, P., and Roe, R. W. (1968). *The application of anthropometry to automotive design.* In Proceedings of Automotive Safety Seminar. Milford, MI: General Motors Corp.

Li, C.-C., Hwang, S.-L., and Wang, M.-Y. (1990). Static anthropometry of civilian Chinese in Taiwan using computer-analyzed photography. *Human Factors, 32,* 359–370.

Lippert, S. (1958, June). The engineering approach to the human factors problems of jet transport aircraft. Remarks prepared for the Panel on the Jet Age and Chest Medicine, 24th Annual Meeting of the American College of Chest Physicians, San Francisco, California.

Lippert, S. (1965). *Estimated body dimensions of the adult male Jewish population of Israel* (TAE Report 40). Haifa: Technion-Israel Institute of Technology.

Lohman, T. G., Roche, A. F., and Martorell, R. (1988). *Anthropometric standardization reference manual.* Champaign, IL: Human Kinetics Books.

Majoros, A. E. (1990). *Simulation protocols for anthropomorphic models* (Douglas Paper 8507). Presented at Workshop on Human-Centered Design for Concurrent Engineering, Wright-Patterson Air Force Base, OH, September.

Manary, M. A., Schneider, L. W., Flannagan, C. C., and Eby, B. H. (1994). *Evaluation of the SAE J826 manikin measures of driver positioning and posture* (SAE Tech. Paper 941048). Reprinted from *Human factors: Lighting, mirrors, and user needs* (SP-1033). Warrendale, PA: Society of Automotive Engineers.

Martin, R. (1928). *Lehrbuch der Anthropologie* [Textbook of anthropology]. (2nd ed.). Jena, Germany: Fischer Verlag.

Martin, R., and Knussman, R. (1988). *Anthropologie: Handbuch der Vergleichenden Biologie des Menschen* [Anthropology: Handbook of comparative human biology]. Vol. 1. Stuttgart: Gustav Fischer Verlag.

Martin, R., and Saller, K. (1957). *Lehrbuch der Anthropologie.* Stuttgart: Gustav Fischer Verlag.

McConville, J. T., Alexander, M., and Velsey, S. M. (1963). *Anthropometric data in three-dimensional form: Development and fabrication of USAF height-weight manikins* (Tech. Documentary Report AMRL-TDR-63-55). Wright-Patterson Air Force Base, OH: Aerospace Medical Research Laboratory, Behavioral Sciences Laboratory.

McConville, J. T., Churchill, T. D., Kaleps, I., Clauser, C. E., and Cuzzi, J. (1980). *Anthropometric relationship of body and body segment moments of inertia* (Tech. Report AFAMRL-TR-80-119). Wright-Patterson Air Force Base, OH: Aerospace Medical Research Laboratory.

McConville, J. T., and Laubach, L. L. (1978). Anthropometry. In *Anthropometric source book. Volume I: Anthropometry for designers* (NASA Reference Publication 1024). Houston: NASA Scientific and Technical Information Office.

McConville, J. T., Robinette, K. M., and Churchill, T. D. (1981). *An anthropometric data base for commercial design applications* (Phase I, Final Report, NSF Grant DAR-8009861). Yellow Springs, OH: Anthropology Research Project, Inc.

McConville, J. T., Tebbetts, I., and Alexander, M. (1979). *Guidelines for fit-testing and evaluation of USAF personal-protective clothing and equipment* (AMRL-TR-79-2). Wright-Patterson Air Force Base, OH: Aerospace Medical Research Laboratory.

McFarland, R. A., Domey, R. G., Duggar, B. C., Crowley, T. J., and Stoudt, H. W. (1968). *An evaluation of the ability of amputees to operate highway equipment* (Report RD-592). Boston: Harvard School of Public Health.

McHenry, R. R., and Naab, K. N. (1966). *Computer simulation of the automobile crash victim in a frontal collision — a validation study* (CAL Report YB-2126-V-1R). Buffalo, NY: Cornell Aeronautical Laboratory.

Meindl, R. S., Zehner, G. F., and Hudson, J. A. (1993). *A multivariate anthropometric method for crew station design (statistical techniques)* (AL/CF-TR-1993-0054). Wright-Patterson Air Force Base, OH: Aerospace Medical Research Laboratory.

Meldrum, J. F. (1965). *Automobile driver eye position* (SAE Paper 650464). Warrendale, PA: Society of Automotive Engineers.

Mitutoyo. (1992). Mitutoyo measuring instruments (Catalog 9000). Paramus, NJ: MTI Corp.

Mood, A. M. (1950). *Introduction to the theory of statistics.* New York: McGraw-Hill.

Moss, J. P., Coombes, A. M., Linney, A. D., and Campos, J. (1991). Methods of three dimensional analysis of patients with asymmetry of the face. *Proceedings of the Finnish Dental Society, 87*(1), 47–53.

Moss, J. P., Linney, A. D., Grinrod, S. R., Arridge, S. R., and Clifton, J. S. (1987). Three-dimensional visualization of the face and skull using computerized tomography and laser scanning techniques. *European Journal of Orthodontics 9,* 247–253.

Najjar, M. F., and Rowland, M. (1987). Anthropometric reference data and prevalence of overweight, United States, 1976–1980. *Vital and Health Statistics* (Series 11, No. 238). Hyattsville, MD: National Center for Health Statistics.

NASA (National Aeronautics and Space Administration). (1986). *Man-systems integration standard, Volume I* (NASA-STD-3000). Houston: Author.

Norkin, C. C., and White, D. J. (1985). *Measurement of joint motion: A guide to goniometry.* Philadelphia: F.A. Davis Co.

Obergefell, L. A., Gardner, T. R., Kaleps, I., and Fleck, J. T. (1988). *Articulated total body model enhancements, Volume 2: User's guide* (Tech. Report AAMRL-TR-88-043). Wright-Patterson Air Force Base, OH: Aerospace Medical Research Laboratory.

Penny and Giles. (1991). Sales brochure. Blackwood, England: Author.

Pheasant, S. (1986). *Bodyspace — Anthropometry, ergonomics and design.* London: Taylor & Francis.

Philippart, N. L., and Kuchenmeister, T. J. (1985). *Describing the truck driver's workspace* (SAE Paper 852317). Warrendale, PA: Society of Automotive Engineers.

Philippart, N. L., Roe, R. W., Arnold, A., and Kuchenmeister, T. J. (1984). *Driver selected seat position model* (SAE Paper 840508). Warrendale, PA: Society of Automotive Engineers.

Raab, S., Fraser, G., Muhlhan, G., Hochstadt, B., and LaCoursiere, L. (1991). *Metrecom user manual.* Lake Mary, FL: Faro Medical Technologies, Inc.

Reynolds, E., and Lovett, R. W. (1909). A method of determining the position of the center of gravity in its relation to certain bony landmarks in the erect position. *American Journal of Physiology, 24,* 289–293.

Reynolds, H. M. (1977). *A foundation for systems anthropometry* (Report 770911). Wright-Patterson Air Force Base, OH: Air Force Office of Scientific Research.

Reynolds, H. M., Freeman, J. R., and Bender, M. (1978). *A foundation for systems anthropometry. Phase II* (UM-HSRI-78-11). Ann Arbor, MI: University of Michigan, Highway Safety Research Institute.

Reynolds, H. M., and Hubbard, R. P. (1980). Anatomical frames of reference and biomechanics. *Human Factors, 22,* 171–176.

Rioux, M. (1989). Computer acquisition and display of 3-D objects using a synchronized laser scanner. In *Three dimensional media technology, Proceedings of the 1989 International Conference* (pp. 253–268), Montreal, Quebec.

Roe, R. W. (1993). Occupant packaging. In J. B. Peacock and W. Karwowski (Eds.), *Automotive ergonomics — Human factors in the design and use of automobiles* (pp. 11–42). London: Taylor & Francis.

Roe, R. W., and Hammond, D. C. (1972). *Driver head and eye position* (SAE Report 720200). Warrendale, PA: Society of Automotive Engineers.

Roebuck, J. A. (1957). Anthropometry in aircraft engineering design. *Journal of Aviation Medicine, 28,* 41–56.

Roebuck, J. A. (1965). *Knob torque strength requirements for space suit glove operation.* Master's thesis, University of California at Los Angeles.

Roebuck, J. A. (1976). *Aerospace benefits to engineering anthropometry* (Rockwell International Paper SD 76-SH-0093). Presented at 6th Congress of the International Ergonomics Association, College Park, Maryland, July.

Roebuck, J. A. (1989, June). *Engineering anthropometry applications to industrial ergonomics.* Presented at Industrial Ergonomics and Safety Conference, Cincinnati, OH.

Roebuck, J. A. (1991). Overcoming barriers to computer human modeling for concurrent engineering. In E. Boyle et al. (Eds.), *Proceedings of Design for Maintainability, a Workshop* (pp. 8–30). Wright-Patterson Air Force Base, OH: Armstrong Laboratory, Human Resources Directorate, Logistics and Human Factors Division.

Roebuck, J. A., Kroemer, K. H. E., and Thomson, W. G. (1975). *Engineering Anthropometry Methods.* New York: Wiley. (Available from the author or University Microfilms, Ann Arbor, MI.)

Roebuck, J., Smith, K., and Raggio, L. (1988). Forecasting crew anthropometry for shuttle and space station. In *Proceedings of the Human Factors Society 32nd Annual Meeting* (pp. 35–39). Santa Monica, CA: Human Factors and Ergonomics Society.

Rogers, S. P. (1976). *Anthropometric data application manikin (ADAM).* Santa Barbara, CA: Author.

Rogers, R. A., and Silver, J. N. (1968). Elements of an effective child restraint system. In *Proceedings of 12th Stapp Car Crash Conference Detroit* (pp. 172–187). Warrendale, PA: Society of Automotive Engineers.

Sanders, M. S. (1977). *Anthropometric survey of truck and bus drivers: Anthropometry, control reach and control force.* Washington, DC: Department of Transportation, Bureau of Motor Safety.

Sanders, M. S., and Shaw, B. E. (1985). *U.S. truck driver anthropometric and truck work space data survey: Sample selection and methodology* (SAE Tech. Paper 852315). Warrendale, PA: Society of Automotive Engineers.

Santschi, W. R., DuBois, J., and Omoto, C. (1963). *Moments of inertia and centers of gravity of the living human body* (AMRL TDR 63-36). Wright-Patterson Air Force Base, OH: Aerospace Medical Research Laboratory.

Schneid, T. D. (1993). *Americans with Disabilities Act.* New York: Van Nostrand Reinhold.

Scott, W. R. (1991, June 24). Computer simulations place models of humans in realistic scenarios. *Aviation Week and Space Technology,* pp. 64–65.

Severy, D. M., Brink, H. M., and Baird, J. D. (1968). Vehicle design for passenger protection from high speed rear-end collisions (Paper 680774). In *Proceedings of 12th Stapp Car Crash Conference Detroit* (pp. 94–163). Warrendale, PA: Society of Automotive Engineers.

Sheldon, W. H., Stevens, S. S., and Baker, W. B. (1940). *The varieties of human physique.* New York: Harper and Brothers.

Siegel, A. W., Nahum, A. M., and Appleby, M. R. (1968). *Injuries to children in automobile collisions* (SAE Report 680771). Warrendale, PA: Society of Automotive Engineers.

Snow, C. C., Reynolds, H. M., and Allgood, M. A. (1975). *Anthropometry of airline stewardesses* (Department of Transportation Report FAA-AM-75-2). Oklahoma City: Federal Aviation Agency, Office of Aviation Medicine, Civil Aeromedical Institute.

Snow, C. C., and Snyder, R. G. (1965). *Anthropometry of air traffic control trainees* (Report AM 65-26). Oklahoma City: Federal Aviation Agency, Office of Aviation Medicine, Civil Aeromedical Institute.

Snyder, R. G. (1970a). *Human impact tolerance* (SAE Reprint 700398). Warrendale, PA: Society of Automotive Engineers.

Snyder, R. G. (1970b). Occupant restraint systems of automotive, aircraft and manned space vehicles: An evaluation of the state of the art and future concepts. In E. S. Gurdjian et al. (Eds.), *Impact injury and crash protection* (pp. 496–561). Springfield, IL: Charles C Thomas.

Snyder, R. G., Spencer, M. L., Owings, C. L., and Schneider, L. W. (1975). *Physical characteristics of children as related to death and injury for consumer product safety design* (Final Report UM-HSRI-BI-75-5). Ann Arbor: University of Michigan, Highway Safety Research Institute. Prepared for Consumer Product Safety Commission.

Society of Automotive Engineers. (1967). *Passenger car driver's eye range* (SAE Recommended Standard J941a). Warrendale, PA: Author.

Society of Automotive Engineers. (1990). *1990 SAE handbook, Volume 4, on highway vehicles and off road highway machinery.* Warrendale, PA: Society of Automotive Engineers. Contains SAE Recommended Practices, as follows: Devices for use in defining and measuring vehicle seating accommodation, SAE J826
Motor vehicle dimension, SAE J1100
Motor vehicle driver's eye range, SAE J941
Motor vehicle driver and passenger head position, SAE J1052
Accommodation tool reference point, SAE J1517
Driver selected seat position, SAE J1517
Driver hand control reach, SAE J287
Motor vehicle fiducial marks, SAE J182
Describing and measuring the driver's field of view, SAE J1050
Truck driver stomach position, SAE J1522.

Stoudt, H. W., Crowley, T. J., McFarland, R. A., Ryan, A., Gruber, B., and Ray, C. (1970). *Static and dynamic measurements of motor vehicle drivers* (Report HS-800 261). Washington, DC: U.S. Department of Transportation.

Stoudt, H. W., Damon, A., McFarland, R., and Roberts, J. (1965). *Weight, height, and selected body dimensions, United States 1961–62* (Series 11, No. 8). Data from National Health Survey, May 1965. Hyattsville, MD: U.S. Department of Health and Human Services, National Center for Health Statistics.

Swearingen, J. J. (1953). *Determination of centers of gravity of man.* Oklahoma City: Department of Transportation, Federal Aviation Administration.

Swenson, L. S., Grimwood, J. M., and Alexander, C. C. (1966). *This new ocean — A history of Project Mercury* (NASA SP-4201). Washington, DC: U.S. Government Printing Office.

Tebbetts, I., McConville, J. T., and Alexander, M. (1979). *Height/weight sizing programs for women's protective garments* (AMRL-TR-79-35). Wright-Patterson Air Force Base, OH: Aerospace Medical Research Laboratory.

Tilley, A. R. (1994). *The measure of man and woman — Human factors in design.* New York: Watson-Guptill.

U.S. Air Force. (1968, May 1). Cockpit basic dimensions, fixed wing. *AFSC design handbook, 2-2.*

U.S. Department of Defense. (1989). *Human engineering design criteria for military systems, equipment and facilities* (MIL-STD-1472D). Washington, DC: Author.

U.S. Department of Defense. (1991). *Military handbook, anthropometry of U.S. military personnel (metric)* (DOD-HDBK-743A). Natick, MA: U.S. Army Natick Research and Development Labs.

Vannier, M. W., Yates, R. E., and Whitestone, J. J. (Eds.). (1993). Electronic imaging of the human body. In *Proceedings of a Working Group on Whole Body Imaging,* March 1992. Dayton, OH: CSERIAC, Defense Logistics Agency.

Vicinus, J. H. (1962). *X-ray anthropometry of the hand* (AMRL TR 62-111). Wright-Patterson Air Force Base, OH: Aerospace Medical Research Laboratory.

Warren, C. G., and Valois, T. (1991). *Functional categories of persons with disabilities and operational dimensions for designing accessible aircraft lavatories.* Prepared for Paralyzed Veterans of America, National Easter Seal Society, National Multiple Sclerosis Society and United Cerebral Palsy Associations. Seattle, WA: Sponsor.

White, R. M. (1978). Anthropometry and human engineering. In *Yearbook of physical anthropology 1978* (vol. 21, pp. 42–62). New York: American Association of Physical Anthropologists.

Young, J. W., Chandler, R. F., Snow, C. C., Robinette, K. M., Zehner, G. F., and Lofberg, M. S. (1983). *Anthropometric and mass distribution characteristics of the adult female* (FAA-AM-83-16). Oklahoma City: Civil Aeromedical Institute, Federal Aviation Administration.

Zehner, G. (1986). Three-dimensional summarization of face shape. In *Proceedings of the Human Factors Society 30th Annual Meeting* (p. 206). Santa Monica, CA: Human Factors and Ergonomics Society.

Zehner, G., Deason, V., Ervin, C., and Gordon, C. (1987). *A photographic device for the collection of anthropometric data on the hand* (Tech. Report NATICK/TR-87/044). Natick, MA: U.S. Army Natick Research, Development and Engineering Center.

Zehner, G. F., Meindl, R. S., and Hudson, J. A. (1993). *A multivariate anthropometric method for crew station design* (abridged; AL-TR-1992-0164). Wright-Patterson Air Force Base, OH: Aerospace Medical Research Laboratory.

Zeigen, R. S., Alexander, M., Churchill, E., Emanuel, I., and Velsey, S. (1960). *A head circumference sizing system for helmet design* (WADD Tech. Report 60-631). Wright-Patterson Air Force Base, OH: Wright Air Development Division, Aerospace Medical Division.

Appendix A

GLOSSARY

Acromion: An anatomical name for the bony prominence at the top of the shoulder joint.

Anterior: Pertaining to the front surface of the human body or a direction from the depth midplane toward the front.

Beta: See *Veta.*

Buck: The terminology for mockup in the automotive industry.

Clavicles: The bones that extend outward to the shoulder from the center of the chest just below the neck. Muscles of the back and chest region act on these bones to raise and lower the shoulders and move them forward and backward.

Correlation: A statistical concept describing how one measurement varies with respect to another. If the coefficient of correlation is -1 or $+1$, the variability is exactly proportional. If the coefficient of correlation is zero, the variables are independent. Most body dimensions have a coefficient of correlation with one or more other dimensions that is between -1 and $+1$ and only rarely have the value of zero.

Design center of rotation: Another name for *effective center of rotation* for joints. A simplified single point or single axis approximation to the actual instantaneous center of rotation that varies as the joint changes posture.

Dorsal: Pertaining to the back of the body or one of its parts (on the hand, its top surface is opposed to its palmar surface; see Gordon et al., 1989b).

Ear-Eye Plane (or *Line*): An optional plane for defining the orientation of the head for measurements or for defining lines of sight. The Ear-Eye Plane passes through one ear hole and the external canthi of the eye. The *Ear-Eye Line* is the edge view of the Ear-Eye Plane that appears as a line in a side view of the head.

Ectomorphic: A type of body build characterized by relatively little fat or muscle, as compared with the average, and often with small bones and a thin chest. (See also *Somatotype.*)

Effective center of rotation: (also called *Design center of rotation*). The theoretical center of rotation of a joint that meets a number of criteria for location that make it useful for modeling postures. In particular, when the body segments are in appropriate standard anthropometric measuring postures, the segments are in correct position such that certain key external dimensions are accurately represented, such as Buttock-Knee Length, Knee Height, and Stature.

Endomorphic: A type of body build characterized by relatively large amounts of soft, fatty tissue, a large belly, and often relatively less muscular tissue than the average. (See also *Somatotype.*)

Epicondyle: A name for the bony eminence at the distal end of the humerus, radius, and femur (Gordon et al., 1989b). At the elbow and knee, the epicondyles lie approximately on the axis of flexion of the joint.

Eyellipse: An ellipsoidal volume within which is located the range of positions for design eye points for vehicle drivers. This term is a coined phrase used for standards in the automotive industry.

Flesh link: A distance measured from an effective center of rotation of a joint or from a theoretical line between such effective joint centers of rotation to the surface of the skin or clothing of a human body.

Frankfort Plane (also spelled *Frankfurt* Plane). The standard horizontal plane or orientation of the head (Gordon et al., 1989b). It passes through the right tragion (approximate ear hole) and the lower edges of the two orbits (bony eye sockets). In standard measurement descriptions "in the Frankfort Plane" means that this plane is horizontal and the head reference points described above have the defined relationship to the plane. The plane is often used to define angles of the line of sight.

Iliac crest: The highest point on the bony structure of the human pelvis, near what is considered the waist. It may be felt by pressing the thumbs inward and downward at about the mid-depth of the abdomen.

Lateral: Lying near or to the sides of the body, as opposed to medial. Also, the direction of motion away from the centerline of the body (plane of symmetry).

Lateral femoral epicondyle: A bony protrusion at the outside of the knee joint, which is usually close to the effective center of joint rotation, as seen from the side view.

Lateral humeral epicondyle: A bony protrusion at the outside of the elbow joint, which is usually close to the effective center of joint rotation, as seen from the side view.

Lateral malleolus: The bony protrusion at the outside of the ankle.

Link: A name used for the theoretical distance between effective joint centers of rotation. The name is borrowed from mechanical engineering concepts for describing machinery in terms useful for analysis.

Medial: Lying near or toward the medial plane of the body, as opposed to lateral, which is away from the medial plane.

Medial malleolus: The bony protrusion at the inside of the ankle.

Medial Plane: The midplane of the body as seen from the front or back — a plane of body symmetry — that divides the body into a left and right half. Also called in much of the literature the *midsagittal plane.*

Mesomorphic: A type of body build characterized by relatively predominant muscular tissue and heavy bones, as compared with the average. The chest is often called "barrel shaped." (See also *Somatotype.*)

Midsagittal plane: A more commonly used name for the *medial plane.*

Monte Carlo generation or process: A way of randomly selecting a variety of items within a set (body measurements in this context) such that the selection is constrained by the correlations between the dimensions. As used in anthropometric modeling, the goal is to synthesize a set of dimensions that have approximately the same means, standard deviations and correlation coefficients as the sample of measurements from which they were generated.

Multivariate analysis: Statistical analysis methods involving several variables that vary together in a correlated manner. Among these are *principal component analysis* and *Monte Carlo* generation processes.

Omphalion: An anthropological name for the navel.

Percentile: The measurement with a rank value expressed in terms of where it stands in relation to other dimensions from smallest to largest in a population. The fifth percentile is larger than 5% of the other measurements.

Posterior: Pertaining to the back side of the human body, or the direction away from the front of the body. Opposite of *anterior.*

Principal component analysis: A multivariate statistical analysis method that seeks to determine those dimensions that have the greatest influence on the design of specific work spaces and clothing and to organize the data in terms of non-correlated, orthogonal presentation of variability. It also provides a method for describing sets of dimensions for multiple variables (boundary conditions) lying on the border of a set of data defined to encompass a specified percentage of the population.

Reuleaux method: A graphical/mathematical method for determining apparent centers of rotation of moving objects in two dimensions. Identified points on a part are located on each of several successive positions of the part as it moves along the path of motion. Each point is then connected with straight lines and the perpendicular bisectors of each connecting line are defined. The intersections of such bisectors are considered as centers of arcs which describe approximately circular paths of motion of the measured reference points (see Dempster, 1955).

Sagittal Plane: Any plane that is parallel to the plane bisecting the body into a left and right half.

Seating buck: The automotive terminology for a limited mockup of an automobile body or cab containing the seats and main driving controls.

Secular: A term pertaining to historical events, such as changes in average stature of a population over time.

Somatotype: A classification of body build, involving the type of tissues that seem to predominate, general shape characterization, and secondary indications of skin type, hair, and so forth. Many schemes have been devised, but the most commonly used is that of Sheldon, Stevens, and Baker (1940), with three main groups. These groups, called *Mesomorphic, Endomorphic,* and *Ectomorphic,* are defined elsewhere in this glossary.

Trochanterion or *Trochanteric:* The anthropometric name for the bony prominence at the side of the hip. It is a portion of the femur bone of the upper leg. Normally the trochanteric landmark is at the top surface of the bone and is considered very close to the height of the center of rotation of the hip joint.

Veta: An alternate spelling for the statistical term *beta,* which is used for describing measures of the shape of a normal probability distribution (skewness and kurtosis). This spelling was preferred by Edmund Churchill, who wrote, "When we have occasion to spell out the symbol [beta: Greek character], we have used 'Veta' in accordance with contemporary Greek pronunciation" (Clauser et al., 1972).

Appendix B

Illustrations of Anthropometric Dimensions

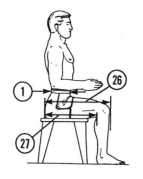

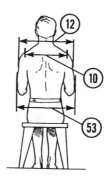

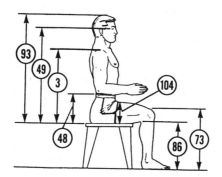

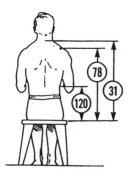

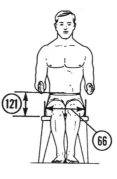

(1) ABDOMINAL EXTENSION DEPTH, SITTING
(3) ACROMIAL HEIGHT, SITTING
(10) BIACROMIAL BREADTH
(12) BIDELTOID BREADTH
(26) BUTTOCK-KNEE LENGTH
(27) BUTTOCK-POPLITEAL LENGTH
(31) CERVICALE HEIGHT, SITTING
(48) ELBOW REST HEIGHT
(49) EYE HEIGHT, SITTING
(53) FOREARM-FOREARM BREADTH
(66) HIP BREADTH, SITTING
(73) KNEE HEIGHT, SITTING
(78) MIDSHOULDER HEIGHT, SITTING
(86) POPLITEAL HEIGHT
(93) SITTING HEIGHT
(104) THIGH CLEARANCE
(120) WAIST HEIGHT, SITTING (NATURAL INDENTATION)
(121) WAIST HEIGHT, SITTING (OMPHALION)

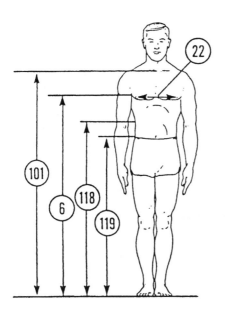

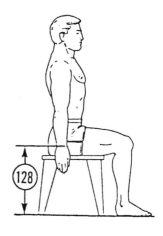

(6) AXILLA HEIGHT
(22) BUSTPOINT/THELION-
BUSTPOINT/THELION BREADTH
(83) OVERHEAD FINGERTIP REACH,
STANDING
(84) OVERHEAD FINGERTIP REACH,
EXTENDED
(85) OVERHEAD FINGERTIP REACH,
SITTING
(101) SUPRASTERNALE HEIGHT
(118) WAIST HEIGHT (NATURAL
INDENTATION)
(119) WAIST HEIGHT (OMPHALION)
(128) WRIST HEIGHT, SITTING

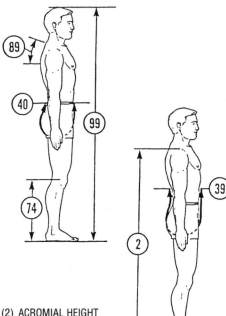
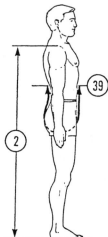

(2) ACROMIAL HEIGHT
(14) BISPINOUS BREADTH
(37) CHEST HEIGHT
(39) CROTCH LENGTH
(NATURAL INDENTATION)
(40) CROTCH LENGTH
(OMPHALION)
(67) ILIOCRISTALE HEIGHT

(74) LATERAL FEMORAL
EPICONDYLE HEIGHT
(79) NECK-BUSTPOINT/
THELION LENGTH
(89) SCYE DEPTH
(99) STATURE
(102) TENTH RIB HEIGHT
(112) WAIST BREADTH

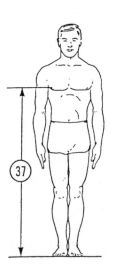
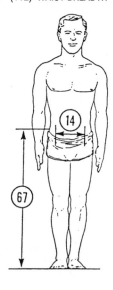

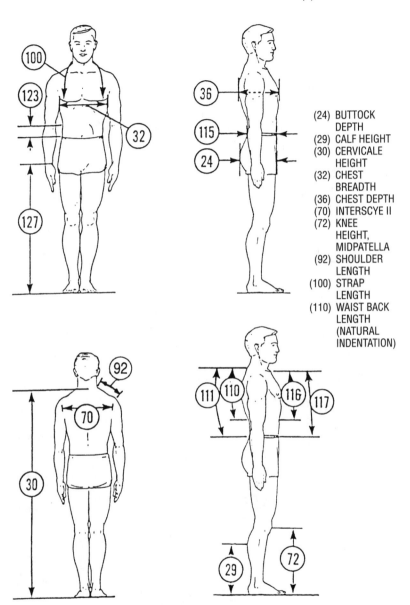

(24) BUTTOCK DEPTH
(29) CALF HEIGHT
(30) CERVICALE HEIGHT
(32) CHEST BREADTH
(36) CHEST DEPTH
(70) INTERSCYE II
(72) KNEE HEIGHT, MIDPATELLA
(92) SHOULDER LENGTH
(100) STRAP LENGTH
(110) WAIST BACK LENGTH (NATURAL INDENTATION)

(111) WAIST BACK LENGTH (OMPHALION)
(115) WAIST DEPTH
(116) WAIST FRONT LENGTH (NATURAL INDENTATION)
(117) WAIST FRONT LENGTH (OMPHALION)
(123) WAIST (NATURAL INDENTATION) TO WAIST (OMPHALION) LENGTH
(127) WRIST HEIGHT

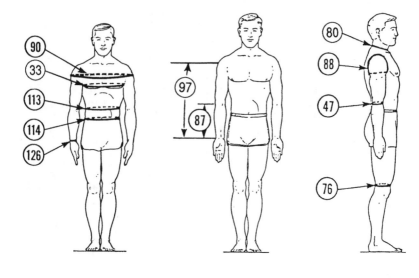

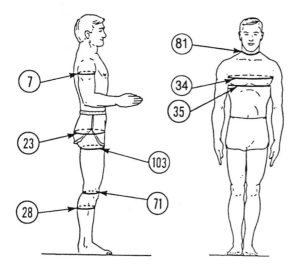

(7) AXILLARY ARM CIRCUMFERENCE
(23) BUTTOCK CIRCUMFERENCE
(28) CALF CIRCUMFERENCE
(33) CHEST CIRCUMFERENCE
(34) CHEST CIRCUMFERENCE AT SCYE
(35) CHEST CIRCUMFERENCE BELOW BREAST
(47) ELBOW CIRCUMFERENCE
(71) KNEE CIRCUMFERENCE
(76) LOWER THIGH CIRCUMFERENCE
(80) NECK CIRCUMFERENCE
(81) NECK CIRCUMFERENCE, BASE
(87) RADIALE-STYLION LENGTH
(88) SCYE CIRCUMFERENCE
(90) SHOULDER CIRCUMFERENCE
(97) SLEEVE OUTSEAM
(103) THIGH CIRCUMFERENCE
(113) WAIST CIRCUMFERENCE (NATURAL INDENTATION)
(114) WAIST CIRCUMFERENCE (OMPHALION)
(126) WRIST CIRCUMFERENCE

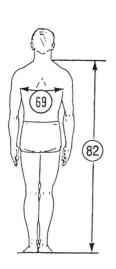
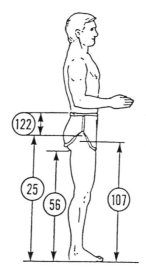
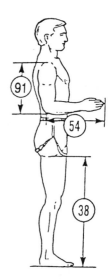
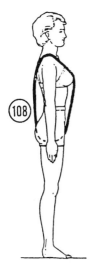
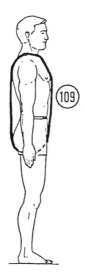
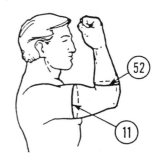

(11) BICEPS CIRCUMFERENCE, FLEXED
(25) BUTTOCK HEIGHT
(38) CROTCH HEIGHT
(52) FOREARM CIRCUMFERENCE, FLEXED
(54) FOREARM-HAND LENGTH
(56) GLUTEAL FURROW HEIGHT
(69) INTERSCYE I
(82) NECK HEIGHT, LATERAL
(91) SHOULDER-ELBOW LENGTH
(107) TROCHANTERIC HEIGHT
(108) VERTICAL TRUNK CIRCUMFERENCE
       (ASCC)
(109) VERTICAL TRUNK CIRCUMFERENCE
       (USA)
(122) WAIST-HIP LENGTH

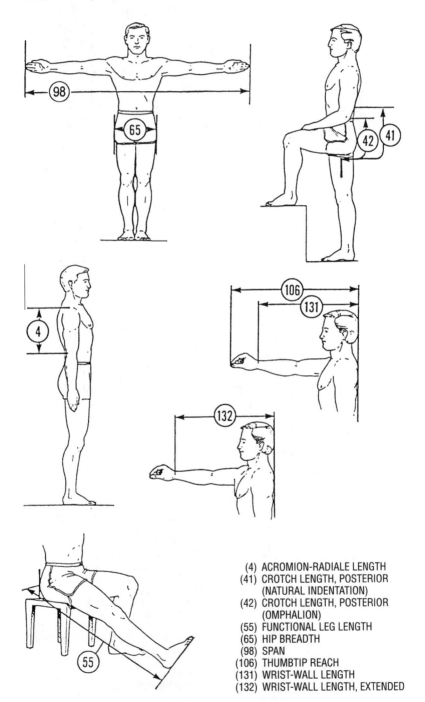

(4) ACROMION-RADIALE LENGTH
(41) CROTCH LENGTH, POSTERIOR
(NATURAL INDENTATION)
(42) CROTCH LENGTH, POSTERIOR
(OMPHALION)
(55) FUNCTIONAL LEG LENGTH
(65) HIP BREADTH
(98) SPAN
(106) THUMBTIP REACH
(131) WRIST-WALL LENGTH
(132) WRIST-WALL LENGTH, EXTENDED

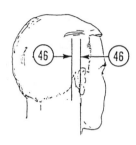

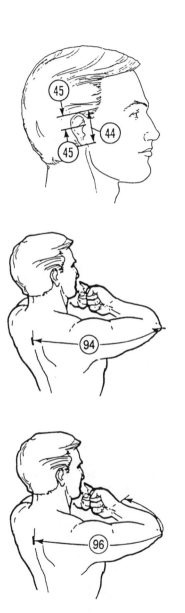

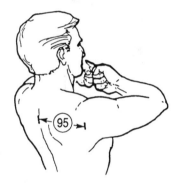

(44) EAR LENGTH
(45) EAR LENGTH ABOVE TRAGION
(46) EAR PROTRUSION
(94) SLEEVE LENGTH, SPINE-ELBOW
(95) SLEEVE LENGTH, SPINE-SCYE
(96) SLEEVE LENGTH, SPINE-WRIST

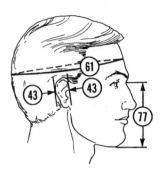

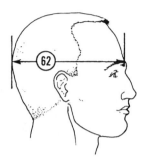

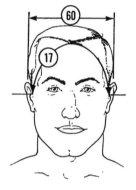

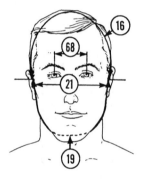

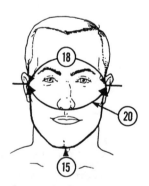

(15) BITRAGION CHIN ARC
(16) BITRAGION CORONAL ARC
(17) BITRAGION CRINION ARC
(18) BITRAGION FRONTAL ARC
(19) BITRAGION SUBMANDIBULAR ARC
(20) BITRAGION SUBNASALE ARC
(21) BIZYGOMATIC BREADTH
(43) EAR BREADTH
(60) HEAD BREADTH
(61) HEAD CIRCUMFERENCE
(62) HEAD LENGTH
(68) INTERPUPILLARY BREADTH
(77) MENTON-SELLION LENGTH

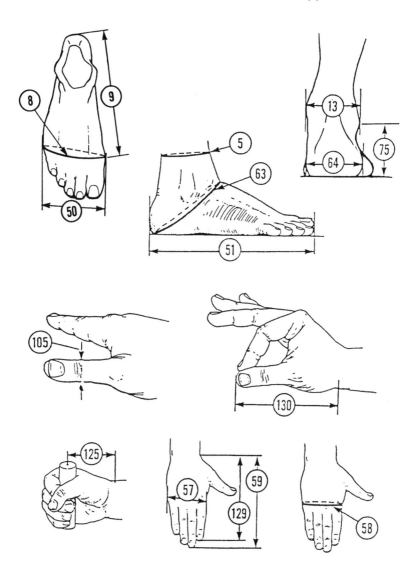

(5) ANKLE CIRCUMFERENCE
(8) BALL OF FOOT CIRCUMFERENCE
(9) BALL OF FOOT LENGTH
(13) BIMALLEOLAR BREADTH
(50) FOOT BREADTH, HORIZONTAL
(51) FOOT LENGTH
(57) HAND BREADTH
(58) HAND CIRCUMFERENCE

(59) HAND LENGTH
(63) HEEL ANKLE CIRCUMFERENCE
(64) HEEL BREADTH
(75) LATERAL MALLEOLUS HEIGHT
(105) THUMB BREADTH
(125) WRIST-CENTER OF GRIP LENGTH
(129) WRIST-INDEX FINGER LENGTH
(130) WRIST-THUMBTIP LENGTH

Selected Dimensions of U.S. Citizens

The following tables summarize data reported on the anthropometric survey of civilians in the United States by the Department of Health and Human Services (Stoudt et al., 1965). Although neither as recent nor as complete as desired, these data indicate the general magnitude of civilian dimensions and their variability. They are representative of the real problems faced by designers and anthropometric analysts today. These tables may be used to illustrate general principles in student projects involving exercises in design, estimating, and forecasting.

TABLE C-1
Dimensions of U.S. Civilian Males, 1960–62 per Health Examination Survey

| No. | Dimension Name | Mean | Std. Dev. | Percentiles and Normal No. of Standard Deviations from Mean | | | | | | | | |
				1st -2.326	5th -1.645	10th -1.282	25th -0.674	50th 0	75th 0.674	90th 1.282	95th 1.645	99th 2.326
1	Height (in)	68.21	2.71	61.6	63.7	64.8	66.5	68.4	70.1	71.7	72.6	74.5
2	Weight (lb)	165.10	27.83	110.3	123.8	131.6	145.7	163.1	182.4	201.7	214.0	238.6
3	Biacromial Diameter	15.61	0.83	13.4	14.1	14.4	15.0	15.7	16.3	16.8	17.1	17.7
4	Right Arm Girth	11.27	1.66	8.1	8.9	9.3	10.1	11.1	12.3	13.6	14.5	16.1
5	Chest Girth @ Scye	39.08	3.08	32.4	34.1	35.1	36.8	38.9	41.2	43.4	44.8	47.4
6	Waist Girth	34.91	4.52	26.8	28.3	29.4	31.6	34.6	37.9	41.0	43.0	46.6
8	Sitting Height, Rel.	34.01	1.45	30.3	31.6	32.2	33.1	34.1	35.1	36.0	36.5	37.5
9	Sitting Height, Erect	35.61	1.45	31.8	33.2	33.8	34.7	35.7	36.7	37.5	38.1	39.1
10	Knee Height	21.32	1.14	18.4	19.4	19.9	20.6	21.4	22.1	22.9	23.4	24.3
11	Popliteal Height	17.31	1.05	14.8	15.4	15.9	16.6	17.4	18.2	18.8	19.2	20.0
12	Thigh Clearance	5.63	0.66	3.9	4.5	4.8	5.2	5.7	6.2	6.7	7.0	7.5
13	Buttock-Knee Length	23.28	1.15	20.5	21.3	21.8	22.5	23.4	24.1	24.8	25.3	26.3
14	Buttock-Popliteal Length	19.43	1.21	16.5	17.4	17.9	18.7	19.5	20.3	21.1	21.6	22.5
15	Seat Breadth	13.93	1.10	11.5	12.1	12.5	13.2	13.9	14.7	15.5	16.0	17.0
16	Elbow-Elbow Breadth	16.53	1.83	12.9	13.8	14.3	15.2	16.4	17.8	19.1	19.9	21.4
17	Elbow Rest Height	9.49	1.18	6.3	7.5	8.0	8.8	9.6	10.4	11.1	11.6	12.4
18	Age	43.24	15.51	18.5	21.1	23.8	31.3	42.2	55.1	66.3	71.9	78.0

Source: Abstracted from Anthropology Research Project staff (1978b)
Note: All dimensions are in inches except Weight, which is in pounds. Dimension 7, Sum of Skinfolds, is omitted.

TABLE C-2
Dimensions of U.S. Civilian Females, 1960–1962 per Health Examination Survey

| No. | Dimension Name | Mean | Std. Dev. | Percentiles and Normal No. of Standard Deviations from Mean | | | | | | | | |
				1st -2.326	5th -1.645	10th -1.282	25th -0.674	50th 0	75th 0.674	90th 1.282	95th 1.645	99th 2.326
1	Height (in)	63.10	2.59	56.9	58.9	59.8	61.4	63.2	64.9	66.5	67.4	69.0
2	Weight (lb)	140.41	30.45	90.3	101.9	107.9	118.9	134.7	156.0	180.8	198.3	236.5
3	Biacromial Diameter	13.95	0.76	12.1	12.7	13.0	13.5	14.0	14.6	15.1	15.4	15.9
4	Right Arm Girth	12.07	1.27	8.1	8.9	9.3	10.1	11.1	12.3	13.6	14.5	16.1
5	Chest Girth @ Scye	34.66	3.20	28.9	30.3	31.0	32.4	34.3	36.6	39.1	40.7	43.7
6	Waist Girth	30.19	4.75	22.8	24.1	24.9	26.7	29.4	32.9	36.8	39.3	44.4
8	Sitting Height, Rel.	32.20	1.51	28.4	29.7	30.3	31.3	32.3	33.3	34.2	34.7	35.5
9	Sitting Height, Erect	33.34	1.43	29.6	30.9	31.6	32.5	33.5	34.4	35.2	35.7	36.5
10	Knee Height	19.56	1.07	17.1	17.8	18.2	18.9	19.6	20.4	21.0	21.5	22.3
11	Popliteal Height	15.63	1.02	13.3	14.0	14.4	15.0	15.7	16.3	17.0	17.4	18.0
12	Thigh Clearance	5.40	0.72	3.7	4.2	4.4	4.9	5.4	6.0	6.6	6.9	7.1
13	Buttock-Knee Length	22.37	1.22	19.6	20.4	20.8	21.6	22.4	23.2	24.1	24.6	25.7
14	Buttock-Popliteal Length	18.89	1.21	16.1	16.9	17.4	18.1	18.9	19.8	20.6	21.1	22.1
15	Seat Breadth	14.44	1.47	11.5	12.3	12.7	13.4	14.3	15.3	16.4	17.2	19.0
16	Elbow-Elbow Breadth	16.53	1.83	12.9	13.8	14.3	15.2	16.4	17.8	19.1	19.9	21.4
17	Elbow Rest Height	9.08	1.15	6.0	7.1	7.6	8.4	9.2	9.9	10.6	11.1	11.9
18	Age	42.61	15.43	18.5	20.9	23.3	30.3	41.7	54.1	65.83	71.1	77.9

Source: Abstracted from Anthropology Research Project staff (1978b)
Note: All dimensions are in inches except Weight, which is in pounds. Dimension 7, Sum of Skinfolds, is omitted.

TABLE C-3
Coefficients of Correlation for Anthropometric Dimensions of U.S. Civilian Males, 1960-1962

		1	2	3	4	5	6	7	8	9	10	11	12	13	14	15	16	17	18
1	Height (in)		.3922	.3764	.1376	.1953	.0653	.0320	.7098	.7627	.7997	.7601	.2021	.7372	.5923	.3093	.0796	.2038	-.2539
2	Weight (lb)	.3922		.4745	.8503	.8848	.8281	.7052	.4545	.4110	.4033	.1490	.6952	.5572	.3849	.8158	.8089	.3100	-.0428
3	Biacromial Diameter	.3764	.4745		.3801	.4184	.2496	.2310	.3363	.3654	.3529	.2756	.3058	.3646	.2531	.3434	.3118	.1278	-.2359
4	Right Arm Girth	.1376	.8503	.3801		.7839	.7118	.6720	.2642	.2199	.1926	-.0604	.6654	.3423	.2243	.6741	.7547	.2684	-.0977
5	Chest Girth @ Scye	.1953	.8848	.4184	.7839		.8378	.6903	.2980	.2384	.2291	.0003	.6078	.3881	.2536	.7322	.8341	.2578	.0789
6	Waist Girth	.0653	.8281	.2496	.7118	.8378		.6964	.1839	.1056	.1371	-.0985	.5388	.3238	.2163	.7164	.8202	.1905	.3005
7	Sum of Skinfolds*	.0320	.7052	.2310	.6720	.6903	.6964		.1860	.1241	.0637	-.1444	.5356	.2458	.1274	.6287	.6525	.2513	.0206
8	Sitting Height, Rel.	.7098	.4545	.3363	.2642	.2980	.1839	.1860		.8726	.4434	.3819	.2823	.4278	.2745	.4215	.2093	.4547	-.1790
9	Sitting Height, Erect	.7627	.4110	.3654	.2199	.2384	.1056	.1241	.8726		.4459	.4100	.2351	.4175	.2275	.3643	.1357	.5439	-.2665
10	Knee Height	.7997	.4033	.3529	.1926	.2291	.1371	.0637	.4434	.4459		.7984	.2240	.7434	.6273	.3099	.1345	-.0294	-.1708
11	Popliteal Height	.7601	.1490	.2756	-.0604	.0003	-.0985	-.1444	.3819	.4100	.7984		-.0315	.6168	.5241	.0483	-.1187	-.0604	-.2184
12	Thigh Clearance	.2021	.6952	.3058	.6654	.6078	.5388	.5356	.2823	.2351	.2240	-.0315		.3491	.2395	.5779	.5995	.2146	-.1899
13	Buttock-Knee Length	.7372	.5572	.3646	.3423	.3881	.3238	.2458	.4278	.4175	.7434	.6168	.3491		.7357	.4497	.2995	.0050	-.1359
14	Buttock-Popliteal Length	.5923	.3849	.2531	.2243	.2536	.2163	.1274	.2745	.2275	.6273	.5241	.2395	.7357		.2649	.1924	-.1447	-.0823
15	Seat Breadth	.3093	.8158	.3434	.6741	.7322	.7164	.6287	.4215	.3643	.3099	.0483	.5779	.4497	.2649		.7069	.2851	.0464
16	Elbow-Elbow Breadth	.0796	.8089	.3118	.7547	.8341	.8202	.6525	.2093	.1357	.1345	-.1187	.5995	.2995	.1924	.7069		.2273	.1688
17	Elbow Rest Height	.2038	.3100	.1278	.2684	.2578	.1905	.2513	.4547	.5439	-.0294	-.0604	.2146	.0050	-.1447	.2851	.2273		-.1842
18	Age	-.2539	-.0428	-.2359	-.0977	.0789	.3005	.0206	-.1790	-.2665	-.1708	-.2184	-.1899	-.1359	-.0823	.0464	.1688	-.1842	

*Two skinfolds: triceps and subscapular.
Source: Churchill et al. (1977)

TABLE C-4
Coefficients of Correlation for Anthropometric Dimensions of U.S. Civilian Females, 1960–1962

	1	2	3	4	5	6	7	8	9	10	11	12	13	14	15	16	17	18
1 Height (in)		.2047	.4081	-.0178	.0388	-.0807	-.0687	.7193	.7636	.7850	.7218	.1368	.6147	.5204	.1501	-.0433	.2348	-.2674
2 Weight (lb)	.2047		.4524	.8891	.8850	.8536	.7484	.1802	.2107	.3304	-.0288	.7028	.6321	.5073	.8102	.8525	.2584	.1985
3 Biacromial Diameter	.4081	.4524		.3325	.4336	.3022	.2426	.3156	.3493	.4062	.2543	.3720	.4265	.3406	.3265	.3326	.0958	-.1151
4 Right Arm Girth	-.0178	.8891	.3325		.8431	.8024	.8094	.0343	.0521	.1277	-.2201	.6425	.4489	.3551	.7465	.8344	.2228	.2778
5 Chest Girth @ Scye	.0388	.8850	.4336	.8431		.8632	.7393	.0440	.0599	.1810	-.1272	.5976	.4406	.3712	.6800	.8791	.1807	.2992
6 Waist Girth	-.0601	.8536	.3022	.8024	.8632		.7187	-.0908	-.0753	.1230	-.1652	.5260	.4090	.3331	.6659	.8708	.1135	.4076
7 Sum of Skinfolds*	-.0807	.7484	.2426	.8094	.7393	.7187		-.0041	-.0070	.0732	-.2380	.5783	.3394	.2736	.6457	.7356	.1812	.2543
8 Sitting Height, Rel.	.7193	.1802	.3156	.0343	.0440	-.0908	-.0041		.9075	.4199	.3530	.1973	.3261	.2300	.1956	-.0309	.5327	-.2736
9 Sitting Height, Erect	.7636	.2107	.3493	.0521	.0599	-.0753	-.0070	.9075		.4398	.3648	.2078	.3462	.2316	.2027	-.0331	.5845	-.3108
10 Knee Height	.7850	.3304	.4062	.1277	.1810	.1230	.0732	.4199	.4398		.7462	.1905	.6879	.5863	.2525	.1044	.0188	-.1172
11 Popliteal Height	.7218	-.0288	.2543	-.2201	-.1272	-.1652	-.2380	.3530	.3648	.7462		-.1433	.4271	.3867	-.1045	-.2031	-.0972	-.1804
12 Thigh Clearance	.1368	.7028	.3720	.6425	.5976	.5260	.5783	.1973	.2078	.1905	-.1433		.4628	.3537	.6098	.5967	.2901	-.0269
13 Buttock-Knee Length	.6147	.6321	.4265	.4489	.4406	.4090	.3394	.3261	.3462	.6879	.4271	.4628		.7860	.5517	.4123	.0498	-.0349
14 Buttock-Popliteal Length	.5204	.5073	.3406	.3551	.3712	.3331	.2736	.2300	.2316	.5863	.3867	.3537	.7860		.3898	.3286	-.0453	.0013
15 Seat Breadth	.1501	.8102	.3265	.7465	.6800	.6659	.6457	.1956	.2027	.2525	-.1045	.6098	.5517	.3898		.6962	.2748	.1869
16 Elbow-Elbow Breadth	-.0433	.8525	.3326	.8344	.8791	.8708	.7356	-.0309	-.0331	.1044	-.2031	.5967	.4123	.3286	.6962		.1429	.3750
17 Elbow Rest Height	.2348	.2584	.0958	.2228	.1807	.1135	.1812	.5327	.5845	.0188	-.0972	.2901	.0498	-.0453	.2748	.1429		-.1550
18 Age	-.2674	.1985	-.1151	.2778	.2992	.4076	.2543	-.2736	-.3108	-.1172	-.1804	-.0269	-.0349	.0013	.1869	.3750	-.1550	

*Two skinfolds: triceps and subscapular.
Source: Churchill et al. (1977)

Index